Power Walk!

Power Walk!

*My Step by Step Journey
to Competitions Across America*

PATRICIA VICARY

Toplight

Jefferson, North Carolina

ISBN (print) 978–1-4766–8675–2
ISBN (ebook) 978–1-4766–4489–9

Library of Congress and British Library
Cataloguing data are available

Front cover image © 2022 Shutterstock/Christian Mueller

Printed in the United States of America

Toplight is an imprint of McFarland & Company, Inc., Publishers

Box 611, Jefferson, North Carolina 28640
www.toplightbooks.com

Acknowledgments

A huge thank you to teacher/editor/memoirist/manuscript sherpa extraordinaire Cat Pleska for the positive feedback and unstinting support that helped to bring this book to life. Cat, you saw the potential in this project before I did and helped me to believe in it too. Thanks to Christine Arvidson for graciously providing an assist in helping me to reach my goal. I also want to express my appreciation to the faculty of Arizona State University's Master of Liberal Studies program, especially Dr. Megan Todd. You provided the original inspiration for this project and helped me feel my writing was worth reading.

I am grateful to the crew at McFarland and Toplight for bringing this project to fruition, notably Susan Kilby and Beth Cox.

A big shout-out to my support team: Training and traveling wouldn't have been anywhere near as much fun without the companionship, gossip, and miles of laughter provided by Kellie Bernardez and Isabel Gomez. Physically enduring all of those miles out on the roads and trails likely would not have been possible without Channing Azzolino and her Absolute Barre program. Jennifer Tubbs, thank you for keeping me walking through the years and for sharing life's ups and downs along the way.

Special thanks to Channing, Jennifer, Sandie Hernbroth, Kathleen Oswalt, Dr. Sam Zizzi, and Jahdai Bolds for contributing their expertise to this project.

Finally and most importantly, I could not have done any of this without the support of my husband and son. Thank you, Todd and Derek, for your patience with the endless hours I spent training and writing and all of those trips away from home in pursuit of my goal. Thanks for putting up with me, guys—I love you.

In memory
of my mother,
who dreamed I'd someday
be a book author

Table of Contents

Preface

Not typically one to be overly concerned about the passage of time, I have to confess that becoming an empty nester in my late 50s was a turning point for me. It felt like a great opportunity to take stock of where I was in my life and, even more important, where I was going. What did I want the next few decades of my life to look like? I didn't have a bucket list of things to do or places to go, but I knew that staying both mentally and physically fit would be important factors in maintaining the ability to do whatever would come next.

Already a committed power walker with an ingrained exercise habit, I decided that addressing mental fitness would be my top priority. That's why I chose to embark on a master's degree in liberal studies at Arizona State University. A project in that program led to blogging and publishing articles about power walking and my travels around the United States to participate in half marathons. The enthusiastic response I received indicated an eagerness for information on power walking and the 50-state challenge; that encouraged me to embark on an oh-so-very 2020 pandemic lockdown project—writing a manuscript.

This book traces my evolution from a non-athlete to a committed exerciser dedicated to sharing the joys and benefits of power walking with others. I begin with the basics, mapping out a strategy for starting, supporting, then sustaining a power walking practice. There's expert advice from professionals in the fields of sports nutrition, psychology, physical therapy, and more. And because I believe that there's no teacher like experience, I share what I've learned through decades of training for countless races from 5Ks to full marathons.

I also share my adventures—the good, the bad, and the embarrassing—that occurred during my quest to complete a half marathon in every state: tales of scary porta-potties, scarier mini-planes, and finish line triumphs. From the most disappointing medals to the best post-race biscuits, you'll find it here.

All of the events portrayed herein are factual, presented from my perspective, and my hopefully not-too-faulty memories. Some names have been changed; a few characters are composites used to indicate encounters over a period of time. I've done my best to re-create conversations as closely as I could recall them; they are paraphrased but not verbatim. Any reference made to a business, service, or product does not imply endorsement. As always, please seek advice from professionals before embarking on any health or wellness plan.

Perhaps you're looking for inspiration that will get you going on a fitness program. Maybe you're considering a switch from your current physical activity to something new or you think you might like to give competition a try. I hope that here you will find information, motivation, and entertainment that will inspire you to reach your own goals, as you discover the health and happiness that can be found within walking distance.

1

Power Walking

A What, Why and How-To Guide

"You *go,* fitness walker lady!"

The competitors at the California International Marathon were a few miles into the 26.2 we'd be covering that morning. An impressive crowd of spectators lined the streets, especially given that the temperature that December day was stuck somewhere well south of frigid. With a pair of snazzy leopard-print gloves rounding out my basic black Lycra power walking gear, I was cruising at a 12:54 pace, attempting to meet a personal time goal—and desperately trying to generate some much-needed body heat.

"You *go!*" the voice rang out again, my frozen face now cracking into a slight smile. I was touched by this overt display of enthusiasm; we back-of-the-pack types usually receive feeble cheers at best. Maybe it was the sight of someone walking a marathon at a rapid pace that drew the woman's eye, maybe it was the gloves ... it might have been my undoubtedly pained facial expression. But hers wasn't the only comment I'd receive during this race. As we hustled toward the finish line after five and a half hours of effort, a pack of slower runners sprinted over to ask me a question.

"We've been taking bets on this and we just gotta know. Did you actually walk the entire race?"

"I sure did," I replied.

They exchanged stunned looks.

"How," the runners shrieked, "is that even possible?!"

Power walking. Fitness walking. Speed walking. Whatever you call it—it's power walking to me—it's a wonderful way to achieve and maintain fitness. It's a non-intimidating, achievable pathway for

3

someone who is currently inactive but wants to start an exercise program. It can be a life-changer for folks who used to run or engage in other high-impact exercise but now want something new due to injuries or other physical limitations. Power walking allows them to exercise indoors on a treadmill or outdoors on trails or roads and even to compete if they choose to do so. Power walking provides many of the same physical benefits as running, such as an elevated heart rate and metabolism. Because it is also a weight-bearing exercise, it can build and maintain the bone density that is so critically important as we age. What it doesn't do is present many of running's risks, including joint stressors that can lead to injury.

Another similarity between power walking and running is that power walkers can participate in the same goal setting, training, camaraderie, and challenges of racing that runners enjoy. Except for a small number of events with very strict time limits, power walkers can be out there competing on the roads and trails with the runners. We earn the same T-shirts and medals and even the same finish line bananas and bagels as the speedier guys and gals.

What Exactly Is Power Walking?

The words power walking sometimes conjure up images from the sport of race walking. Race walkers are those Olympic athletes who can resemble a pack of waddling ducks on an angry rampage. The hip-swinging motion that results from keeping the support leg straight may appear somewhat humorous, but their pace is no joke; elite race walkers can crank out sub-7:00-minute miles.

Power walking is much more relaxed. There are no rules requiring a specific body alignment; it's the same kind of walking you've been doing all your life, done at a faster (or much faster) than normal pace. One exception that differentiates power walking from regular walking is arm action. Most walkers find that as they increase speed their arms will naturally assume a roughly 90-degree angle, ideally at waist level. They become pistons that help to propel the walker's forward movement.

Many slower runners have called out to me as I pass them during races, "You walk faster than I run!" While the fastest power walkers can achieve a top pace of around 11 minutes per mile, most people find that a pace of 12 minutes or under will result in both feet leaving the ground—at which point it's a run, not a walk. The majority of power walkers train and race at a far slower pace. As time goes on, my half marathon race pace has gone from the high 12:00s to the mid–13:00s, and I'm okay with that (or so I tell myself—acceptance of becoming slower is, for me, an ongoing process).

In the Beginning

Nothing in my background would have indicated that I'd someday participate in sports of any kind beyond buying tickets to watch a game. My family's involvement in athletics consisted of my dad yelling at the television while the Detroit Lions lost yet another football game. His aerobic activity was limited to climbing on the roof of the house to adjust the television antenna; if he tweaked it just right, we would pick up a fuzzy signal from an out-of-town station broadcasting the games that were blacked out locally. Familial fandom of the Detroit sports teams didn't translate into any sort of athletic prowess. So how did I, the girl who burst into tears when required to jump a hurdle in junior high, who managed to fail physical education class in high school (yes, it can be done!), end up competing in countless races by choice? Some of the credit, or blame, goes to my elementary school gym teacher Mr. Thornton.

Field Day at Beverly School was a big deal; for most kids it was the high point of the year. We sixth-graders had trained like little aspiring Olympians thanks to Mr. Thornton's coaching. Only the truly uncoordinated can possibly understand the depths of humiliation and fear that comprised my years in gym class under Mr. Thornton's watchful eye: the indignities of dodge ball, the last-place finishes in nearly every contest…. I never even learned to pull off a cartwheel.

But Field Day brought forth a miracle: first-place finishes in not one but two contests. (Sure, they might have been team events, but still!) Holding out my hand to collect that second blue ribbon, even Mr. Thornton was moved to exclaim, "Wow—another one!" So what does it say about me that, now more than 50 years later, I not only clearly remember that moment but still possess those two strips of faded blue satin?

I think it says I have a thing for athletic bling.

My high school graduation brought with it an end to forced athletic torment. I will

Where my bling obsession began.

never forget that realization washing over me; no one could ever make me take a P.E. class again. There would be no more plunges into a cold swimming pool I could at best dog paddle across; no more swinging haplessly at pitched softballs; no more flailing at badminton shuttlecocks. Never again would I be the embodiment of a cliché that for me had been torturous reality: the last girl chosen for the team. Here's a cold, hard truth I learned along the way: The last kid standing isn't actually chosen at all. No, they never say your name; the captain of the side that's stuck with you merely rolls her eyes then leads her team off toward the field of your impending torment as you trail behind, awash in humiliation. I can't express how thrilling it was to know I'd never have to live through that mortification ever again.

If there's one school topic that bedeviled me as much as physical education, it was science. Well, if I'm being honest, math was right up there, too. (What can I say—I was a speech and theater gal.)

6

But while I was smart enough to choose a college that grouped core requirements in a way that allowed me to avoid math, science was another story. When my junior year of college found me desperately searching for a science class that wasn't *too* science-y, I enrolled, with great trepidation, in Foundations of Physical Education. Yes, there was science—twice-weekly kinesiology lectures with three days devoted to so-called lab. The lab subjects? Those would be our bodies, as we ran around the college track or on the local roads. Humiliation surely awaited, but at least no revolting frog dissections would be required.

* * *

"It's a great day to be alive!"

A chorus of groans met the inevitable proclamation from Professor Egnatuk (aka Eggy) as we rounded the track. I stayed with the back-of-the-pack girls while guys from the cross-country team churned their legs at warp speed up front. Exiting the stadium, we'd run to a local park, lungs straining for sufficient oxygen to allow both locomotion and gossip. I had to admit this wasn't so bad. Eggy never made anyone feel less-than; he supported, and exhorted, us equally even though he served as the track coach for those greyhounds. A local woman who seemed downright ancient to us college kids—she was perhaps all of 40 years old—was in our class, also. Peggy wasn't in great physical shape, but she too was made to feel welcome. After that semester ended, I was shocked when I found myself voluntarily going out with friends for runs that were—could it be?—fun.

That new running hobby continued after college. When a co-worker at the hole in the wall radio station where I worked suggested that a group of us enter a 5K race, there was no way I was going to miss out on the fun, even though the thought of it was intimidating. We dubbed our gang the EMTs; this was both an acronym in recognition of our éclair and Mai Tai training regimen and also a nod to our fears of requiring emergency medical aid during the race. Although I tried to play it cool with my friends, I was incredibly nervous at the idea of taking part in this public, timed spectacle of athleticism. The specter of physical torments from the past taunted me; how humiliated would I be if I DNF'ed (Did Not Finish) or, even worse, DFL'ed (finished Dead F'ing Last)?

The race we had chosen was the very definition of a fun run, San Francisco's Run to the Far Side, based on the comic strip by cartoonist Gary Larson. When the big day rolled around, I made an amazing discovery—even at my unimpressive pace, hundreds of people were behind me. Most surprisingly, no one seemed to care! It was a joyous bunch of people gathered to have a good time on a weekend morning without judgment or eye-rolling. We all earned the same shirt, heard the same cheers, ate the same overripe bananas. My fear of humiliation turned to revelation; all that mattered was that I was out there, having fun with my friends—and earning a medal in the process sure didn't hurt.

In the decades since then, participating in races has become an integral part of my life. For many of those years I was a runner, never a fast one, but I was able to plonk around well enough to enjoy everything from countless 5Ks to two half marathons. When my body finally protested in the form of back problems and other injuries, a switch to power walking kept me racing. Whether I'm running or power walking, Eggy's words live on in my mind; any day I'm out there is truly a great day to be alive. As I get older, I may get slower, but the race bling gets bigger and better. Now in my 60s, even as a power walker I have managed a few age-group podium finishes—that means more medals! I still get a buzz every time that ribbon, whether it's an age group award or simply a participant medal, goes around my neck at the finish line.

The Power of Walking—Whether Alone or Together

Of course, it's not all about the bling. Another benefit of racing is the incentive it creates to put in training miles week after week. Sure, we all know that exercise is important for maintaining our health, especially as we age. But realistically, finding the oomph within ourselves to do that day after day, year in and year out can be a challenge. That why entering races can be a highly effective motivational tool; when I know I have something coming up, it's that much easier to drag myself outside so I'm not filled with regret over not having trained well enough when I'm standing on that race day start line.

Another thing that helps is knowing that my friend Isabel will be waiting outside my house twice a week at 7:30 a.m. for a power walk. Up and down the hills of our town, we've talked our way through the challenges of raising kids, solved pretty much all of the world's political problems, and fed countless carrots to the local goats. What makes training together work for us? Convenience (we live near each other), endurance (Isabel's remarkable ability to put up with me early in the morning), and similarity of pace. Even the best of buddies can find it challenging to train with someone who's considerably faster or slower.

Each week I also do a longer, solo power walk, sometimes listening to podcasts or music, often just tuning in to the sounds of nature (while simultaneously looking out for mountain lions). That weekly combination of exercising with a friend plus solitary power walks is what works for me; the key is discovering what works for you. Whether you're a loner by nature, you prefer to run with a pack, or maybe a mixture of both, there's no right or wrong way to go when it comes to training.

If a connection is what you crave, there are some great options available for joining up with other runners and walkers. Sandie Hernbroth, a USTA and RRCA certified coach in Pleasanton, California, believes accompanied training can have a big advantage: "Training with a group creates a community of like-minded people to connect with. Having a connection with others helps to keep people motivated, gives them a sense of belonging and a social outlet." Hernbroth said that she has witnessed the start of many a lasting friendship during her years of conducting group training programs.

For someone new to power walking, the thought of joining a group might seem intimidating, but the good news is that many groups will gladly welcome newbies. "I would encourage that person to seek out a training program that focuses on beginners," said

Hernbroth. "Sign up for a 5K program that teaches the fundamentals and gives them a group of people to meet and hopefully find someone who is their speed." If that seems like too daunting a prospect, "find a one-to-three-mile route to complete three or four times a week. Determine how long you can run or power walk at a conversational pace, then do a recovery walk for one minute, then resume running or power walking." Once a comfort level has been reached with those basics, it's time to seek out a group to join.

Power walking with a pack can provide an additional benefit beyond companionship; studies have shown that people tend to mimic the physical output of those they train with. If you've set a goal of increasing your speed, surrounding yourself with faster friends can help you get there.

What personality type enjoys the group training experience? "I think everyone wants to feel part of a community," said Hernbroth, "but that said it is mainly very social, extroverted people that benefit most." She does know many men and women, though, particularly competitive athletes, who tend to shun group workouts because they prefer to train as they compete—alone. Other power walkers like to use their training time as a way to escape from their hectic lives. "One person shared with me that they like to work out alone because they talk all day for work and they don't want to have to do it when they are working out. It's a time for them to be quiet and calm their brain."

One of the things I love about solo training is the opportunity it gives me for some quiet time to work through arguments in my mind. It's amazing how adept I can be at devising the perfect eviscerating comeback or witty *bon mot* when I'm alone, far surpassing my real-time verbal skills. Even if it's simply in my mind, it's so gratifying to come out on top in every disagreement!

For those who train on their own either by choice or by circumstance, there are myriad online groups offering support communities that can remain strictly virtual or develop into real-world connections. The Half Fanatics, 50 States Half Marathon Club, and other Internet-based organizations offer face-to-face opportunities that include pre-race group photos, club dinners, and even shared accommodations for those looking to lower their race travel expenses. Check out the References chapter of this book for information on these and other organizations that can connect power walkers with like-minded companions.

You might decide to go it alone or maybe you prefer to power walk with a gang. Whether your buddies are in cyberspace or close enough for you to swap Clif Bars, training in the environment that's right for you can help to provide the motivation you need to stick with your program and achieve your goals.

What (Not) to Wear

One day I received a text from my friend Reyna, asking if she could join in on my next training session. I was delighted to have her come along, but when we met up at our local park, I knew right away we were going to have a problem. Reyna looked great in her cotton capris, cute T-shirt, and basic casual shoes; I was sporting my usual Lycra tights, moisture-wicking tech shirt, and running shoes. The discrepancy in clothing choices mirrored the difference in our expectations for the workout. Reyna viewed it as a chance to stroll and chat; I had something more arduous (while still chatting, of course!) in mind.

One of the many great things about power walking is how affordable it is. It requires no specialized, potentially expensive equipment. (Some people choose to power walk on a treadmill at home or in a gym; my focus here is on the great outdoors.) While it is possible to power walk wearing regular clothes and a pair of everyday shoes, it is inadvisable for reasons both physical and psychological. Clothing specifically made for sports participation can prevent chafing or constricted movement that sometimes results from the fabric, seaming, or cut of regular clothes. No matter your age, gender, physical condition, body type, or size, there is workout gear available at every price point that can boost your style while providing the freedom of movement necessary for successful power walking.

Perhaps just as important, making the switch into athletic gear puts you in a different frame of mind; it draws a subconscious line that says you're about to engage in a workout that will in all likelihood produce some sweat. There's something about putting on sharp-looking exercise garb that is very motivating. It's a way of telling yourself, your family, and the world that this is an important part of your day, time you cordon off to give your mind and body the attention they deserve. So it's not a bad idea to devote a few dollars to some wardrobe items that will make your power walk more enjoyable.

Of course, you may find that your closet already contains everything you need for power walking. It helps that athletic apparel has gone from strictly functional to fashionable. Athleisure wear has become fully mainstream and wearing gear that was once restricted to the gym or the track is now the daily wardrobe of choice for many. I tried to adopt this dressed-down fashion philosophy, and while I found it to be incredibly comfortable, it had two drawbacks. The first is that I missed that obvious psychological demarcation between workout time and the rest of my day. The second is that leggings go by another name in my house—Satan's pants. Those stretchy waistbands lull me into believing that there's room for one more spoonful of this or forkful of that. I admire those of you who can wear Lululemons all day and maintain your weight; I'll stick with the built-in warning device that a proper pair of pants provides.

If your power walking practice involves heading outdoors in all kinds of weather, that means being prepared for everything from the hottest sun to the coldest wind, rain, and, yes, even snow. Something to keep in mind is that while power walking may not generate as much body heat as running, you're still going to get warm while you're out there. This is a constant battle for me. I am, by nature, a wimp, and that tendency has worsened as I get older. When I first step outside on a cool day, the feel of those chill winds makes me cringe and I'm tempted to bundle up. But I know not to do that; it's better for me to suffer through the first mile, otherwise that extra layer of clothing will soon feel far too warm, and I'll be cursing the fact I brought it along (and then I'm forced to tie the offending item around my waist, where it will annoy me for the rest of my walk). This is something that is best learned from trial and error, but in general, you want to dress in a way that allows for warming up as your workout goes along.

You might want to consider the purchase of some anti-chafing goop, too. I didn't envision the need for diaper rash ointment at this stage of my life, but it's a great way to deal with the chafing that can occur no matter how carefully I select my clothing. Humid conditions are notorious for bringing about these painful skin abrasions; products such as Body Glide are made for just this situation. Good old petroleum jelly and diaper rash creams are other effective prevention methods that are easy-to locate, cost-effective ways of dealing with the chafing that plagues some power walkers.

Shoes You Can Use

Next, you decide to buy some shoes for your new power walking practice. So off you go to your local running shoe store; good move on your part, opting to head straight to the experts instead of any old store that sells athletic shoes. But you can't help feeling overwhelmed when you come face-to-face with a wall of shoes in crazy color combinations, many from unfamiliar brands. Alongside them are more varieties of socks than you could ever have imagined. Where do you start?

Shoes for power walking are easy to find but difficult to choose. Any store that specializes in running shoes will have a selection that works just as well for power walking; the challenge is finding the shoe that's best for your feet. That's where the services of a professional shoe fitter come in. A seasoned pro such as Fleet Feet's Jahdai Bolds can be an invaluable resource to get you going in the right direction. According to Bolds, the average power walker doesn't need to look for a different shoe than the average runner. "Running shoes offer excellent breathability, light weight, superior cushioning that is designed to last 300–500 miles, and a heel to toe offset that propels you forward with every step you take." The key to walking out the door with that just-right running shoe starts with the most important consideration—fit.

"A good fit should be any walker's priority," said Bolds. Finding your perfect fit is more involved than simply trying a few pairs on for size. Bolds explained that an expert shoe fitter will guide walkers toward their best shoe by starting the fit process with an interview. "We want to know our customer's needs, goals, surface they're walking on, and injury history." Next is a scan that gives the pro a 360-degree view of your feet, allowing them to better judge your size, width, and arch height, as well as foot shape. At that point, human inspection takes over from machine. "We'll want to watch you walk to perform a gait analysis," said Bolds. "What we're looking for is how your ankles and arches perform in motion, compared to when they are static." This is how the shoe fitting expert determines how much stability or structure the power walker needs in their shoes, inserts, and yes ... even socks!

Don't be surprised if you end up purchasing a larger size shoe than you are used to. "Most new walkers wear the wrong size shoe which may cause unnecessary blistering, calluses, loss of toenails, bunions, and even Morton's neuroma [pinched nerve]," said Bolds. "We always recommend allowing for at least a full thumb's width of room in front of your longest toe and the correct width, be it narrow, medium, or wide." In my case, that means wearing size nine power walking shoes; that's at least a full size up from my street shoe size.

Sock selection is equally important and potentially every bit as tricky as deciding on the right shoes. Wool, poly-blend, no-show, ankle, quarter crew ... the choices can be mind-boggling. "A great fitting shoe always begins with a comfortable sock that hugs the foot, wicks moisture, and performs as well as you do," according to Bolds. "A well-fitting cotton-free sock hugs the foot, which reduces friction, moisture build-up, and blistering inside the shoe." That allows feet to perform without overcompensation—something that may be caused by a blister or callus. One power walker friend of mine swears by wool socks and won't wear anything else; I'm okay with any sock as long as it's not a no-show, which tends to slip down to my heel. I avoid wearing anything with annoyance potential; if that means looking a little dorky in quarter-crew socks, I'm okay with it. Then there are those folks who wear no socks at all—unimaginable to me, but it's all about personal preference.

Paying attention to fit can go a long way toward preventing power walking injuries. "The most common injury we encounter is plantar fasciitis; Achilles' tendinitis, patella tendinitis, and blistering are other common foot and lower leg issues we come up against," noted Bolds. "A great fitting shoe allows our feet to function more naturally, while still having the support they need." Shoe inserts are another method of preventing and treating injuries, by redistributing pressures along the feet and using proprioception to align the foot within the shoes.

If you find your new shoes haven't performed well, leading to discomfort or even pain, running stores tend to have very generous 10- to 60-day windows for returns and exchanges. For example, Fleet Feet's 2021 policy allowed customers to exchange or return shoes for any reason within the first 60 days of purchase. If a customer's shoes didn't work out well for them once they were out on their training walks, they were invited back for a second or even third chance for the store to make it right.

How will you know when your shoes have gone the distance? An easy way to keep track of shoe mileage is to upload your workouts to a website such as Strava that will not only track the miles per pair of shoes but can even send out an email alert when it's time to shop for a new pair.

The Agony of the Feet and the Toenails

Discussion about socks and shoes inevitably turns to what goes inside them—specifically, feet. And toenails. And also, it must be said, a lack of toenails.

An injury that I suffered more than once back in my running days was the dreaded stress fracture—in my case, of the metatarsal bones in the foot. I'm happy to say that fractures haven't been an issue in my years of power walking. That's likely attributable to several factors: the reduced stress that power walking places on the bones (while still providing plenty of the bone-building benefits of a weight-bearing workout), taking it slowly when increasing weekly mileage (it's a good idea to limit mileage increases to no more than 20 percent per week), and the avoidance of hard surfaces such as concrete whenever possible.

On the rare occasions that I endure a pedicure, I apologize to the technician in advance lest they be overcome with shock. No matter how well my shoes fit it's inevitable that I end up with bruised toenails. While some power walkers will never have this problem, others will experience blackened or even detached toenails no matter what shoe they wear, especially if they incorporate downhill terrain into their program. Although toenail issues can be caused by a too-tight toe box, they can also result from the natural position the individual's feet assume on elevation descents. Kudos go to whoever invented purply-black nail polish—it works wonders at hiding those bruised nails.

Bruised toenails have another unfortunate side effect: the possibility of developing fungal infections, something that I know from personal experience is highly resistant to treatment (I've tried them all, from prescription medications to funky folk cures such as Vicks VapoRub). In a situation such as this, nothing substitutes for the knowledge of a foot care clinic or a podiatrist, particularly one who specializes in athletic issues. I have even resorted to a permanent partial toenail removal on one toe; knowing that nail removal is rumored to be a method of torturing war prisoners caused me to put that particular procedure off until it was my sole remaining treatment option. While it wasn't fun, it also wasn't nearly as bad as it sounds. I was never going to have a career as a foot model anyway, so the short-term discomfort I experienced was worth trading for pain-free feet.

Running recovery shoes and sandals hit the market several years ago with a promise to provide relief to the aching feet of power walkers during the hours of the day when they are not training. They range in appearance from thongs and slides (that even I, a non-fashionista, would not be caught dead wearing in public) to closed-toe shoes that resemble typical running gear. More important than looks, of course, is what they can do for tired feet. They offer arch support that can help to alleviate fatigue and soreness. Many people love them and consider them an essential part of their fitness practice; I find them awkward and a bit painful. This is one piece of optional equipment for power walkers that you have to try for yourself to determine if it works for you. Other methods of providing relief to sore, tired feet and legs are compression socks and stretching exercises.

When Injuries Happen—Physical Therapy for Power Walkers

Participating in power walking or any other athletic activity requires the building and maintenance of the physical scaffolding necessary to achieve fitness goals. Through years of running and figure skating (something I took up for fun as an adult), I've developed my share of lingering injuries that threaten to tear that scaffolding down. Sciatica, hamstring pulls, little meniscus tears ... even nagging shoulder and neck problems from too much time spent on the computer. There are so many types of physical therapy available for minor injuries and those stubborn problem areas that won't seem to go away. Consulting with a medical practitioner is always a recommended first step, and the treatment suggested can involve any combination of physical therapy, chiropractic, acupuncture ... and sometimes that word all physically active people dread—rest.

Conventional physical therapy hasn't always provided me with relief from those problems, but I'm somewhat mistrustful of treatments that seem kind of "out there" even though I try to keep an open mind and give nearly anything a try. One acupuncturist even blamed my lack of improvement on what he labeled my negative mindset toward his treatment methods. (My response? "If it had worked, I'd believe in it.")

When a friend suggested I check into a relatively unknown treatment called myofascial release therapy (MFR), I was skeptical. Very skeptical. My limited knowledge of myofascial release stemmed from several painfully unsuccessful encounters with foam rollers. Some people swear by foam rollers; I swear *at* them. Treatment options are a lot like fitness programs—if you don't like it, you're a lot less likely to stick with it. It took a second recommendation from a physical therapist for me to give MFR a try. Did it work? The proof is in the results; years of regular treatments have helped me to continue pursuit of my fitness goals.

Initially, I didn't understand fascia and the role it plays in our bodies. Jennifer Tubbs, PT, an advanced instructor of fascial fitness in Livermore, California, explained, "Fascia consists of the soft connective tissues in your body. When you pull the skin off of a chicken, there is that shiny stuff that connects the muscle to the skin—that is part of the fascial system." For anyone lacking experience with raw poultry, another way to think of fascia is that it's similar to that transparent plastic wrap you keep in your kitchen.

According to Tubbs, fascia is there to hold everything together, allowing tissues to slide and glide; that sets the stage for movement. It also provides support for joints and organs, aiding nutrients and healing materials to reach cells and facilitating the removal of waste.

As with so many things in life, getting stuck isn't good; when it happens to fascia it can lead to dysfunction. "As we age, we often feel stiffer and less mobile," said Tubbs. "We tend to spend more time sitting; even if we're exercising, we tend to perform activities with decreased impact and more linear type movements. We often decrease the variance of movement, so tissues are generally moved in a smaller range of motion." That means less stretching of the tissues; when the tissues don't move, they stick. Sticking leads to pain and injury, something MFR can fix.

MFR sessions begin with what I call the "Zen-out"—a therapist places their hands on various parts of the client's body, "listening" to get a sense of where the source of the injury lies. Once the problem spot is identified, the practitioner's hands might barely move for several minutes, then there's a sudden release movement. Surprisingly, the spot that requires focus may not be the area where the client is experiencing difficulty.

For example, one of the myofascial chains runs from the bottom of the foot through the back of the leg to the gluteus muscles and into the back. From there it continues to the base of the skull and finally the forehead. Should any part of that chain get strained, injured, or scarred, it can inhibit proper function. That means a stiff back may be a byproduct of a problem in the calf or hamstring.

While I'm a convert to MFR, it's not completely understood by traditional medicine: in part because few studies have been conducted, in part because treatment varies from one therapist to another. I'll admit MFR seemed somewhat strange to me, but in the days following treatment, I experience fewer of my usual aches and movement restrictions. (The hot rock massage at the end of the session isn't bad, either.)

Along with injury treatments that are provided by professionals, there are products on the market that go beyond what the typical over-the-counter pain medications can do. One product in particular that deserves a shout-out is kinesiology tape. These super-stretchy strips can be applied all over the body in various configurations to support weakened areas or reduce pain and swelling without restricting movement. I've used these colorful strips for years to successfully deal with problems such as plantar fasciitis. Consider adding them to your arsenal of weapons to stave off or conquer injury; KT Tape and RockTape are two of the better-known brands. YouTube has an excellent array of videos that show the proper method of application for help with a plethora of problems.

Cross-Training for Power Walkers

Power walkers often discover that, as wonderful as it is, walking alone can't meet all of their fitness needs. But what kind of cross-training works best? It's important to give some love to areas of the body that power walking neglects while strengthening or stretching the spots that become strained by all those miles. And if you can have a little fun in the process, even better.

For several years my cross-training consisted of a few weekly sessions at the gym, where I'd spend 45 minutes on the elliptical trainer before slinging around a few free weights or maybe hitting the weight machines. Over time it became apparent that my hip joints were causing me a lot of pain; my left knee wasn't too happy, either. Despite the discomfort, it was hard to think about giving up a routine I had adhered to for so long, in large part because I was afraid that without that extra cardio, I would start to see my weight creep up. But eventually, common sense prevailed, and I realized that continuing to engage in a cross-training exercise that utilized many of the same movements as power walking did not make for an ideal combination.

What does work well? Yoga, Pilates, and barre classes make excellent complements to a power walking program. There were a few times over the years that I'd given yoga a try. When I worked at a university one of my job perks was free access to the student gym and the many fitness classes it offered. The yoga class I frequented provided a great break from sitting at my desk. But no matter how hard I worked at getting my meditative mindset on, my thoughts always wandered over to the menu at the gym's café and what I'd choose for lunch on my way back to the office. No matter how engaging the instructor, yoga was simply too slow-moving to hold my interest; not only that, it required developing a mastery of precision movement and balance that didn't work well for me. Years later I also made a solid effort at developing a regular Pilates practice. It was a little more mentally stimulating than yoga, but still slower moving than I liked.

So when my current gym offered a free trial barre class—advertised as a combination of yoga, Pilates, dance, and functional training—it already had two strikes against it. Given my general lack of dance experience (it's best to forget my brief flirtations with belly dance and samba) I was less than optimistic but decided I had nothing to lose; I'd give barre a whirl.

As I took a spot in the back of the room, an instructor who looked like Barbie's hot young mom cued up the music and we were off. Wow—barre wasn't boring! The routine took us through balance work, isometric strength training, and stretching. Every part of the body received attention with a constant re-centering on core engagement; even typically neglected areas such as feet and ankles (so crucial to power walkers) were targeted. Weights, straps, a ball, or just our body weight were employed to enhance the movements.

While anyone can benefit from barre, "many of us have lived lives as runners and are used to a high intensity, challenging workout," said Channing Azzolino, a Danville, California, chiropractor who developed the Absolute Barre program. She prescribes barre workouts as rehab for a variety of injuries thanks to barre's non-impact aspect, combined with active stretching that helps to build lean muscles and healthy joints. Barre had another benefit that made it a great fit for me—it works the hips in varied positions to avoid overuse of the straight forward/back leg movement of running and power walking that causes wear and tear over time.

Debate rages on about the advisability of stretching as part of a running or power walking program … before? after? never? Azzolino maintained, "If you stretch properly and maintain muscle length as well as joint range of motion you'll be able to power walk with your body beginning in neutral alignment." Neutral alignment is where the body is the strongest. "It will make every move more efficient and reduce the risk of injuries, both traumatic and repetitive."

When I first made the switch to power walking from my previous running program, my hip flexors sure complained about it. A lot. Power walking uses the hip flexors in a different way than running due to the stride. In running, the back leg provides a lift as the quadriceps contract, straightening that leg and projecting the body up and forward. The front leg has to lift, but not as much as in power walking which lacks this explosive push-off. The hip flexors attach at the lumbar vertebra and will cause lower back pain when tight, spasmed, or injured. Azzolino noted that, "while seated, hip flexors are shortened and will tend, over time, to stay that way. Barre uses both active and passive stretching to specifically target those muscles as well as breathing techniques to alleviate tension."

Of course, I wasn't thinking about any of that as I finished my first class. Instead, I walked out with a very pleasant sense of physical exhaustion—the good kind that comes from working on areas of the body that hadn't received attention in decades, maybe ever. After three classes per week for a few years now, I still look forward to the camaraderie and the energizing music, but most important: I've remained mostly injury-free. I credit that in great part to my new-found strength and flexibility. Barre gives me hope that I can maintain the conditioning that's necessary to reach my goals—not merely in power walking but in staying active throughout my life. I may never look like Barbie's hot young mom, but I'll settle for being a healthy old dame.

Oh, and then there's this: Shortly after my 62nd birthday, I asked the nurse at my annual exam to check my height, afraid that I might have begun losing a little of my already somewhat diminutive "five-three-and-a-half if I stand up super-duper straight" stature. Height loss due in part to spinal compression is considered an inevitable part of the aging process after age 40. But I had to ask her for a remeasure so I could believe her eyes and my ears when she told me I measured in at an even 5'4". I'm not saying that the stretching and lengthening exercises of my barre practice caused me to find that extra half-inch in height I'd always longed for, but hey—I can't prove that it didn't.

No, That Person Over There Is Not Judging You

Colleen and I shared a house in our single gal days; she was tall, willowy … in the lingo of that era, she'd have been termed a total babe. One autumn afternoon she decided to go for a run; clad in loose gray sweatpants and matching baggy sweatshirt, she stood grimacing in front of our full-length mirror. "There's no way I can exercise outside," she moaned. "I'm so fat and flabby. Everyone will see me!" Colleen changed out of her bulky sweats; she never went for that run. Sadly, she's far from the only person I've known who has allowed feelings of unease or anxiety to stand in the way of exercise.

What's the source of so much self-consciousness? Internal focus with its tinge of judgment is the ego; that's according to Dr. Sam Zizzi, Endowed Professor of Sport and Exercise Psychology and Associate Dean for Research at West Virginia University's College of Physical Activity and Sports Sciences. He stated, "Any time we become self-conscious, we disrupt the experience of the moment and instead focus on our train of thought learned throughout our lives. These thinking habits can be quite limiting, keeping people from pursuing certain behaviors." Dr. Zizzi noted that scientific study in the area of exercise anxiety hasn't featured a significant focus on outdoor exercise, concentrating more on indoor exercise and such issues as mirrors in gyms. "I would imagine the likelihood of being judged power walking outside would be less than in a crowded gym," said Zizzi, adding that "ultimately people, especially women, won't walk solo if they don't feel safe outdoors."

Let's say that someone is intrigued by the idea of power walking but feels too self conscious to get started; Zizzi's solution is to take baby steps. "Start in the most comfortable location where the likelihood of being judged is low then eventually work on their own attitude and tolerance for more difficult environments. If someone is working on changing their lifestyle and pursuing mental and physical health, I try to help them realize that guilt and self-consciousness are just self-imposed barriers and these thoughts are not reality." Zizzi's approach is mindfulness-based, a way of viewing thoughts and feelings as things that come and go. "People can learn to be self-aware of these thoughts and they are taught to label them but not identify with them. So they could think anxious thoughts about their body or how they are being judged but not *feel* anxious." Practicing this detachment can help a person to gain some relief from their self-imposed suffering.

Although it's a rare occurrence, I've been on the receiving end of unwanted attention; for example, the guy on a bicycle who yelled, "Fat legs!" at me and then, to ensure I didn't miss out on his critique, circled back to shout it out a second time. Dr. Zizzi's thoughts on harassment are clear; it is unacceptable behavior that no one should have to deal with. "Safety is such an important issue for walking outdoors. Few will walk solo without feeling confident about their personal safety." The foundation for feeling more comfortable starts with safety precautions. At a minimum that means bringing along

23

identification in the form of photo ID or any of the various wearable items such as engraved dog tags or bracelets specifically made for that purpose. A phone can allow for making emergency calls; some power walkers carry a whistle or other noise-making device while others prefer pepper spray. One proven way to make any power walk safer is to turn it into a social occasion that includes others and then sticking to well-traveled areas.

As for dealing with the aftermath of an uncomfortable experience, Zizzi said, "Just because someone is mean towards you does not mean you must feel depressed or anxious. You are not in control of how others act, but you are in control of where you exercise and how you think about what others say." I can't say those few incidents I experienced rolled right off me because I do recall them, but I haven't let those people live in my head rent-free; they never stopped me from doing what I wanted to do. Their commentary says much more about them than it does about me.

My observation is this: Most people aren't actually paying much attention to anyone else. The few who do are likely thinking, *"Wow, good for him/her. Why can't I be that motivated? Ugh…. I need to get out there and get some exercise, too."* We are all so wrapped up in our own lives that we aren't focused on others. Think about what pops into your head when you see someone running or walking. My guess is that you do what most people do, which is to admire their efforts to stay fit no matter their size, age, or physical condition.

What to Eat

It was a typical muggy Michigan summer evening spent hanging out with some college friends when we decided to stop at Howard Johnson's restaurant for a snack. Eagerly digging into my dish of butter crunch ice cream, I consumed every bit of it before it could fall victim to the heat. Apropos of nothing my friend Connie suddenly uttered perhaps the most accurate assessment of my personality I would hear in my entire life.

"You're happiest," she said, "when you're eating."

1. Power Walking

The first thought that crossed my mind wasn't to be offended or embarrassed or even to protest that it wasn't true. No, my thought then and now was, *Well, isn't everyone?*

I suppose I've learned along the way that no, not everyone reaches peak happiness when they are consuming food. I have to admit that even for me, that happiness is often tinged with guilt: I'm eating too much, or more often I'm not eating the right kinds of food. While I have never experienced an eating disorder, I think it's fair to say that I have disordered eating; a lot of my mental energy goes toward food, and I struggle to maintain a balanced, healthy relationship with what I eat.

In other words, I'm hardly one to offer advice to others about nutrition; fortunately, there are experts like Kathleen Oswalt to provide guidance on how to eat right. Oswalt, a Charleston, South Carolina–based registered dietitian nutritionist with an extensive background in sports nutrition, said that the foundation of a healthy diet for power walkers is the same as for everyone: "Focusing on balanced nutrition at mealtime and snack time is ideal. This means the goal is to include all three macronutrients (complex carbohydrates, lean proteins, and healthy fats) along with a variety of fruits and vegetables, plus adequate hydration."

Over the years carbohydrates have picked up a reputation as something to avoid as if they are bad for us. Not so, according to Oswalt. "Complex carbohydrates are a very efficient source of fuel (or energy) and therefore should be the bulk of caloric intake." Another key to a balanced diet? "Moderate amounts of lean protein from either plant-based or animal-based foods are important to not only help build muscle but also help repair tissues and tendons that are broken down in the process of training—and, of course, when you race." Oswalt also emphasized eating a variety of fruits and vegetables in order to access their wide variety of vitamins, minerals, and fiber; along with keeping your mind and body healthy, they help to maintain higher performance levels and speed recovery.

Many people come to power walking as older adults; their nutritional needs can differ from someone younger. "As we age some nutrients become especially important," said Oswalt. "The most notable difference in nutritional needs for the older adult is the increased need for more calcium and vitamin D to help maintain good bone health. Choosing foods higher in calcium is essential for maintaining strong bones." Among her top choices:

- kale, spinach, and collards
- beans and lentils
- soy products like tofu and edamame
- figs
- seeds including sesame and chia
- almonds
- dairy products and fortified non-dairy milks

Oswalt added that calcium supplementation may be needed; if so, it's important to also take the vitamin D3 that's essential for your body to properly absorb calcium.

Consulting with a physician or registered dietitian is recommended to decide if supplementing with vitamin B12 is right for you. "Studies have shown that a small number of people over the age of 50 have a decreased ability to absorb vitamin B12," said Oswalt. "Over time this could cause a deficiency but focusing on vitamin B12-rich foods can help prevent that from happening." She noted that vitamin B12 can be found in all animal products but folks over 50 may discover that incorporating fortified foods into their diet can be very beneficial: "These include some fortified cereals and non-dairy milks as well as fortified nutritional yeast."

I'm certainly not one of those lucky souls who can eat anything and everything they want yet feel great and not gain weight. But regular exercise goes a long way toward allowing me to eat a little of the less-nutritious stuff that keeps me happy while still leaving room for a (mostly) healthy diet. Those extra few hundred calories I burn off every time I power walk let me feel I've earned the occasional (in all honesty, maybe a little more often than occasional) Mexican Coke or chocolatey indulgence.

Making the Move from Exercise to Athlete— Power Walking a Race

Many power walkers are perfectly content to put in their miles simply as a form of exercise, a way of getting out in nature, and spending time with friends. But many of us get the bug to race as a way of maintaining motivation ... or adding to our T-shirt collection. If training for a race appeals to you, a quick online search will turn up any number of training plans. The References section at the end of this book also suggests a few sources that provide excellent guidelines for power walk race training. I've been using the same plan for so many years I don't recall where it came from; I only know that it worked for me and if it ain't broke...

So what's the plan? Three days a week of power walking; my usual Tuesday/Thursday route clocks in at just under five miles, while on the weekend I stretch that out to six. When I was entering half marathons once or twice a year, those six-milers on the weekend became increasingly longer distances until I reached a maximum of 11–12 miles a few weeks before my race. My power walk days alternate with thrice-weekly one-hour barre classes; one day a week is devoted to recuperation. The weekly rest day is a concept that I'm happy to say is fully sanctioned by my physical therapist.

Many experts suggest walking 13–14 miles a few weeks prior to a half marathon; it's not the physical miles that are important so much as the psychological confidence that comes from knowing you've covered the full 13.1-mile race distance before and can do it again when the big moment arrives. It's part of a race philosophy best summed up as "don't do anything for the first time on race day." Many a first-time full marathoner has followed a training plan with a maximum distance of 20 miles; when they confront those final six miles during the race it's uncharted territory that can add an unwelcome psychological component to the physical stress they are enduring. In my case, I've completed so many half marathons that I know I can get that distance done so there's no need to add the extra miles in training.

I discovered that when I race often enough, those races substitute for my longer weekend training walks. Once I committed to the

50-state goal, I increased the frequency of my races. They became so close together that it wasn't necessary—or even desirable—to continue with long power walks during training; instead, I kept my non-race weekend walks to six miles. Maintaining this schedule helped me to meet my goal, which was not to PR (set a personal record), but to get through my race schedule injury-free.

When choosing the target race that's right for you, take into consideration your expected pace and how much time you think you'll need to complete the course. Power walkers should look for races that are considered walker-friendly, with a minimum three-hour time limit (that requires you to walk a 13:44 pace) for a half marathon, six hours for a full ... and more is better. It all depends on how much pressure you're willing to endure when faced with a time cutoff. Often the half marathons with the most generous time limits are the events with a simultaneous full marathon; competitors at every race distance are sometimes allowed to stay on the course for the entire time the full marathon is taking place.

If you have a time goal in mind, you might be in search of tips for increasing your pace. I've never tried speed work or other techniques that runners use; my process has always been one of addition and subtraction. The addition is increasing my arm cadence while maintaining the same position—arms near the waist, not down at hip level or with fists swinging up near my face. I keep my shoulders lowered, consciously keeping a relaxed upper body. (Allowing the shoulders to creep up can result in soreness. During long training walks and races, I always do a few shoulder rotations along the way to help me stay loose and limber.)

The subtraction is to eliminate anything that diverts my focus. Unfortunately, that includes chatting with friends during training or races; the more I talk, the slower I go. I also say goodbye to podcasts during training, switching them out for up-tempo music. The difference between the two can be as much as a minute per mile. During a race, staying focused on a minutes-per-mile goal is helpful, as is targeting people ahead of me in the pack that I want to pass or people behind me that I want to keep behind me. That's where pacers can be helpful. They are the folks many races employ to carry signs indicating that they will complete the race in a specific time. Hang with them during the race and you are guaranteed to finish in the given time frame.

Another consideration is the type of race you think you'd most enjoy. Many first-time competitors get a case of pre-race jitters; would yours be calmed by knowing that the field of participants is a small one of between, say, 50 and 200 people? That means there will likely be shorter lines for the porta-potty and fewer logistical issues to juggle. But it also increases the odds you'll be out on the course alone at some point and the race won't have that vibrant ambiance found at big happenings. Conversely, a race with several thousand enthusiastic entrants offers an electric atmosphere and usually some pretty good perks as well; a pre-race expo crammed with vendor booths, upgraded swag (race goodies and souvenirs), and a sense of being part of a Big Deal. But you have to know your tolerance for potential pitfalls such as race day traffic jams, parking shortages, shuttle busses, and more. A good compromise for a first-timer might be an event with 1,000–2,000 racers that combines the best of both worlds, giving you a feel for the type of environment that most appeals to you.

When you're preparing for the Big Day, here's an important tip: Never wear anything for the first time during a race. It's worth repeating that race-day philosophy to not attempt anything for the first time under race conditions. That means no—do *not* succumb to the temptation to wear the official race T-shirt you picked up hours ago at the expo. This is not the time to try out that new sports bra. For the love of blisters, don't wear new socks or shoes! Go with the tried and true, lest you experience chafing or even bleeding that puts an end to your race or results in searing pain in the shower. Not to mention that many racers believe it's bad form or even bad karma to wear the tee before you've completed the race. I'm not superstitious, but why tempt fate?

A race day food plan is important for races in your local area, and even more so when traveling to an event. According to sports dietitian Kathleen Oswalt, "The main idea is to make sure you don't go into your event fasting. You'll need to fuel and hydrate your body pre-event for the best results. You'll also want to make sure you fuel during your event and then nourish and replenish nutrient losses after." As with everything else race-related, the Big Day is not the time to try something new; stick with the food you've been eating during training. Digestive distress makes for memorable experiences, but those aren't the kind of memories anyone wants.

There are a variety of training meals that Oswalt believes also work well before competition:

- cold cereal with milk (dairy or non-) and fruit
- pancakes or waffles with nut or seed butter
- yogurt or non-dairy yogurt with berries and nuts
- oatmeal and your choice of milk with fruit and nuts
- English muffin, bagel, or toast with nut or seed butter
- egg with toast or plain white potatoes

These meals are easy to digest and provide the energy needed to start your race strong. Personally, I'm a big fan of the yogurt/fresh berries combo: easy to pull off at home, but a hotel minifridge makes it possible on road trips as well. When refrigeration is not an option, I've settled on eating two KIND breakfast protein bars while I wait for the gun to go off; they feature a good mix of carbs and protein.

It's not only food that's important; fluids are also key. "Don't forget to hydrate!" warned Oswalt. "Make sure you go into your event hydrated, especially if it looks like it will be a hot day. Aim for 16–32 ounces of fluid a couple of hours before your event." This, my friends, is why porta-potty access is a consideration when choosing races. "Once your event is completed your hydration doesn't stop there," Oswalt continued. "You'll want to make sure you replace fluids lost through sweat. Hydrate with water, and electrolytes if needed, to help with recovery."

For power walkers, food is a concern not only before but also during their race. Oswalt stressed that when it comes to fueling during your event it's best to consume foods that are low in fat, higher in carbs. "Carbohydrates are your body's preferred source of fuel; although fat is an important macronutrient it can be harder to digest and possibly cause gastrointestinal upset." She suggested carrying snacks that are high in carbohydrates with a small amount of protein for satiety. And practice makes perfect even when it comes to race-day snacking; make sure to do a trial run of eating and hydrating before race day. "It's easy to get distracted and be ultra-focused out on the course; this could lead to under-fueling and dehydration because you forgot to eat and drink. If you need to set your watch to remind you to take some sips and a few nibbles, do it."

Some race directors are great about providing food along the course and even before a race, while at other races you're lucky to get some GU (little packets of energy gel) or an orange slice with your water. For mid-race munchies, I like to carry a small box of raisins plus a little bag of almonds; they are lightweight and fit easily in a pocket. "If you're participating in a longer distance where you're walking for hours or you have back-to-back events in one weekend, you may want to have a variety of snacks and sports nutrition options with you in case flavor fatigue sets in," suggested Oswalt. She proposes a mixture of sweet and savory flavors that can help with palatability when you're not really feeling like fueling in the middle of a race.

A word to the wise: Consume those mid-race snacks when you are in the vicinity of an aid station that has fluids available. There's nothing that will put you off your pace faster than having a stray bit of food stuck in your throat with nothing available to wash it down (ask me how I know). Also, give some thought to the weather forecast and how your snack of choice will hold up under those conditions. It's no fun to pull out that energy bar you've been dreaming of for the last few miles only to discover that all the yummy chocolate goodness has morphed into an inedible brown blob.

You've put yourself through a lot; post-race is the time to show your body some love. Oswalt shared ideas on the best way to do that. "Once your event is over it's beneficial to consume a small snack within 15 minutes to enhance the recovery process. This is especially important if you have events on successive days." Oswalt's ideal mini-meal would contain both carbohydrate and protein; examples include:

31

- a LÄRABAR
- chocolate milk
- a smoothie
- a banana or apple combined with nut or seed butter

I'm Team Chocolate Milk all the way on this one.

Then comes the real post-race meal, that well-earned nosh that's both replenishment and celebration. "Within two hours of completing your event make sure to eat a well-balanced, nutrient-dense meal," suggested Oswalt. "It should include all three macronutrients as well as vegetables and/or fruit." If you have another race the next day, she said, "the main focus is to make sure you're extra diligent about nourishing, refueling, and hydrating your body. This will ensure that you minimize the effects of under-fueling or dehydration and will maximize performance."

In the end, Oswalt said that food choice before, during, and after competition depends on the person and their individual needs or preferences. "Every power walker is different; thus their nutrient needs will be slightly different. Sometimes it takes trial and error to figure out what's going to keep you feeling energized, giving you strength and stamina. Ensuring your body is adequately nourished and fueled is essential to having the energy you need to power walk strong to the finish line." Although I may not always make perfect food selections, I try to keep in mind that perfection is the enemy of good. The memory of crossing finish lines with energy to spare motivates me to make smart food choices more often than not.

Happy Trails (and Paved Roads) to You

My mom always told me it's not polite to discuss money. Forgive my lack of manners, but racing—and especially traveling to races—can be an expensive proposition. While power walking itself may be one of the least expensive sports out there, race registration fees and accompanying expenses can add up over time. But there are ways to make racing more affordable.

1. Power Walking

One way to keep expenditures in check is to join a running club that offers registration discounts (see the References section of this book for details). Many races also offer tiered sign-up fees to encourage participants to register well in advance. While committing early can save money, be sure to check the refund/referral policy before signing up. Some race directors offer refunds, but it's more typical for them to give an opportunity to roll the registration over to a different race or the same event the following year. Occasionally there's the option to sell/transfer the registration to another person, or there's no alternative but to walk away and lose the money. It's not that they are inflexible; race directors have to pay for city permits, advertising, medals, and race shirts often well in advance. The registration fees you pay may already have been spent by the time you request a refund.

A few times when traveling out of state for work-related reasons I found local races to attend or locations that required me to pay for just one additional leg of airplane travel. I tried to book the same airlines, hotel chains, and rental car companies every time I could to take advantage of member discounts. But beware of discount airlines that have reputations for late arrivals, bumping passengers, and flight cancellations; if you're traveling the day before your race, an offer to get you to your destination first thing the next morning won't help unless you plan to parachute directly from that plane to the start line of your race.

I know many dedicated athletes who willingly sleep in tents or cars to feed their racing travel appetite. While I am in awe of their dedication, I made the decision that my safety and comfort are paramount; past travel experiences involving cockroaches, blood-stained bedding, and dicey strangers have made a lasting impression. On some of my out-of-state race trips, I have been joined by my friend Kellie (helpful for both camaraderie and splitting of expenses) or my husband Todd. But when traveling alone I opt to stay in hotels; motel room doors often face parking lots or courtyards where anyone can see that a person is entering their room alone. That's a safety risk any woman traveling alone might want to think twice about taking.

What Makes You Move

Your alarm goes off. It's still dark outside; the sun won't be making an appearance for a while. Or maybe not at all—a glance at the weather app on your phone shows that rain is expected throughout the morning. Your bed is toasty warm ... and one more precious hour of sleep would feel soooo good.

But so would a power walk. It's simply a different kind of good. The kind of good that makes you feel switched on physically, mentally, emotionally.

And so you get up. On goes your workout gear; you take time to eat or drink a little something. It's starting to get a little bit light out now as you step outside. Yeah, there's a light rain falling, but that's okay. You're not made of sugar; you're not going to melt. A few minutes into your power walk and you can feel that you've loosened up, your muscles have warmed a bit, the lingering overnight creakiness has been smoothed out of your joints. Now your mind follows suit, awakened yet calmed by the steady rhythm of your footsteps on the pavement. Maybe it's meditative for you, or perhaps this is your problem-solving time, or the time in your day when you do your best creative work. Whatever it is, it's all good. This is your time.

Where do power walkers find their motivation to get out of bed to exercise or to carve out time for themselves during or after a busy day? What inspires them to keep up an exercise routine day after week after month after year?

Motivation and inspiration are similar animals with a crucial difference. They can start (or keep) someone on the path to fitness. Motivators are often described as external forces, while inspiration comes from within. While I think that's true to some extent, I define my fitness motivations as stemming from the avoidance of a negative. I'm motivated to exercise because I'm afraid of gaining weight. I fear growing unhealthy and infirm in my old age. I think about my late father, a physically active man who stayed mentally sharp into his 90s. My mother, on the other hand, never cared for exercise; in her later years, she succumbed to dementia. Was the difference in their mental health related to their physical activity? I'm not sure but do know that I plan to follow my father's example.

I have other motivators for power walking that are more positive, such as spending time outdoors to soak up sunshine and creating that all-important vitamin D in the process. But more than anything else, outpacing my demons is what motivates me to keep moving.

Inspiration is a different story. Inspiration is what I feel when I look at the racks of race participation medals in my home. I recall how good it felt to earn them; there's something inside me that craves a repeat of that high. I think about the fulfillment of setting and achieving my exercise goals. Inspiration happens when I read stories about the positive role that power walking or running has played in someone's life. It happens when I watch a film about running—I have yet to find one about power walking (any budding filmmakers out there want to take a crack at it?). Every book and film that appears in the References section of this book has inspired me to continue doing what I do.

Somewhere in the middle of the Portland Marathon back in 2002, I encountered an older woman power walking as we crossed the Burnside Bridge. Chatting for a few moments as we motored along, she mentioned that she was 80 years old and tried her best to participate in the race every year. I was struck by the joy she radiated, her true happiness at being a part of the day no matter what her pace or any pains she may have been suffering. Two decades later I remember her so clearly because she represents everything I hope to be at her, or any, age. She was inspirational in her enthusiasm; so are the thousands of other people I have raced with or come across on training walks throughout the years. A handful I have met, most I never will. But I am endlessly inspired by the community of runners and walkers who hit the roads and trails to train and by those who gather at a start line ready to give that race their best shot.

Along a race course there are usually inspirational signs—some funny, some encouraging, some unintentionally deflating (no, we are *not* "almost there" at Mile 9 of a half marathon, thank you very much). But my all-time favorite sign is the one that reads:

35

Power Walk!

One day you won't be able to do this.
Today is not that day.

I think of that aphorism at some point during every race and quite often during my training walks as well. Sure, there will likely be some day I won't be able to do this. But every day that I can, even if it's raining or cold or I'm tired or grouchy, I'm thankful, thankful to be out there power walking and grateful for every benefit it brings.

2

50 States
and Washington, D.C.

Half Marathon Races and Places

Completing a half marathon in every state? To me, that was an incomprehensible goal that would only cross the mind of an over-achiever, some lifelong athlete who relished the idea of suffering through an ultra-marathon or Ironman triathlon. Certainly, it wasn't meant for someone like me, a mom in her mid–50s who had stopped running years before and now power walked the occasional half marathon close to home. Oh yeah, and it certainly wasn't meant for someone who hates to fly—and as a West Coast resident, traveling around the country for races would most certainly involve consider-able amounts of air travel.

But that was then.

Although the 50-state bug didn't strike at my first out-of-state race back in 2013, it wasn't too long before an off-hand comment from a friend set me off on a cross-country journey to do just that.

2013
California
Washington, D.C.

California

A WHOLE BUNCH OF 'EM, 1993–2016

There's no way I'd try to recall all 41 (and counting) half marathons I've done in California dating back to the prior millennium. But the medals I've earned over that period tell a story of how the marketing efforts of half marathons have changed over the years.

My first half, the 1993 Three Valleys Half in Pinole, didn't offer a medal—that would rarely happen today, when many competitors rate races based on the finisher's bling. But Race #2, the San Diego Marathon, handed out what was considered a snappy medal for its time: not round but a rectangle. Pretty hot stuff for 1994!

Medals remained fairly traditional for the next

The height of mid '90s medal chic.

several years, such as the one from the See Jane Run race in Alameda. This contest helped to usher in the era of "chick runs," nominally female-exclusive races that featured such supposed enticements as the chocolate and champagne referenced in the medal design. My personal experience is that neither substance is particularly appealing when you're dehydrated and wrung out after a race, which may be why they've been replaced by beer as the race director's refreshment of choice.

With the "you go, girl!" era in full swing, the

I prefer to power walk for chocolate milk.

races (and swag) became bigger and brassier, exemplified by the Diva race series. Tiaras and pink boas were distributed around Mile 12 for *vogueing* across the finish line, where participants received oversized, bedazzled bling. Here we marked the apex of "mullet dressing"—business up top, party down below in the form of stiff, glittery tutus worn by a large percentage of competitors. Had I ever become lost on a race course, I would only have needed to follow the trail of glitter on the ground to find my way back. I made a race tutu once but never wore it; not only did it feel incredibly scratchy, I knew I'd never get the sparkly stuff off my car upholstery.

Not all of the chick races went for big bling ... some, such as the late, great Nike Women's Race Series, offered Tiffany necklaces that doubled as medals. Participants crossing the finish line were greeted by hunky guys in tuxedos bearing silver trays stacked high

The bling gets bling-ier.

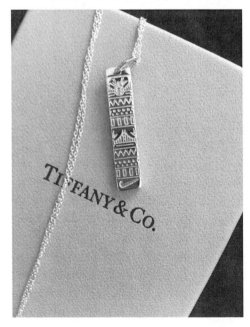

with Tiffany boxes, each containing a custom sterling silver charm on a chain.

Local races can't be expected to offer the same level of bling as those underwritten by a mega-corporation like Nike ... and they don't. Here's where I differ with others over what constitutes a cool race medal. While some people love a bold design, I prefer a traditional small round medal to an immense thing featuring

Nike Women's Race 2014 medal.

40

cartoonish characters. As enjoyable as Northern California's Brazen Racing series is (well-organized fun with a family atmosphere), to me the medals—ranging from scary animal heads to freaky octopi to babies blasting off into space to (my least favorite) this kilt-wearing, bagpipe-playing, largemouth bass—appear to have been designed by someone in the throes of a particularly bad nightmare.

Top notch race series, but this medal...

There was also a brief phase in medal design that I think of as the kitchen implement years. Race directors apparently arrived at a telepathic mutual agreement that medals should do double duty as coasters or bottle openers. I prefer my medals to function solely as medals; I don't need them to chop my onions. For example, the upper three-quarters of the design depicting the marquee of Oakland's Fox Theater is one of my all-time favorites. But things go all wrong with that upside-down shoe-shaped bottle opener at the bottom. I am happy to report that this particular phase ended before participants were blessed with glitzy sporks on satin ribbons.

Best of all were the medals that gave a sense of where the race took place, such as the one from the San Jose Rock 'n' Roll event that incorporated elements from the California license plate and the state flag plus the date.

I'll close with a medal that sums up the "place where it happened" vibe perfectly. The medal from San Francisco's U.S. Half Marathon

Left: **It's a medal, it's a bottle opener … it's complicated.** *Above:* **Indeed, I do know the way there.**

is split into two halves. One side shows a rendering of a cable car; the halves can then be spun to show the other side's design of the Golden Gate Bridge (which participants cross not once but twice). Set off by a rivet-like detail that runs along the medal's frame and presented in the scarlet and gold tones associated with both the bridge and the city, it's a medal that simply couldn't be awarded anywhere else in the world.

Washington, D.C.

Nike Women's Half Marathon

In 2013 the idea of completing a half marathon in every state, or even any state other than California, hadn't crossed my mind. I was content to merely pick up races here

Left and right: **Clever medal with rotating dual design.**

and there when a location seemed appealing or maybe it offered a cute T-shirt or fun medal. Up to that point I'd taken my racing show on the road twice, for full marathons in Oregon and British Columbia. So how did I find myself signing up for a half marathon on the other side of the country? Perhaps not surprisingly, it was the lure of irresistible bling ... a finisher's medal in the form of a Tiffany necklace.

As a veteran of several Nike events close to home, I knew what a great race they put on. These supposedly women-only shindigs (although men were known to participate) featured top-notch race shirts, fanatical fields of runners and walkers, and, best of all, those necklace medals. When Nike announced that they were extending their race series beyond San Francisco for the first time, I couldn't sign up fast enough for the inaugural race in Washington, D.C.

Everything was as well-organized as expected from Nike. Despite the crowd (this race was a sell-out), packet pickup at the expo was a breeze. That might have been because Nike was one of the

43

few organizations that didn't hand out race shirts up front. Instead of including them along with other pre-race necessities such as bibs (also known as race numbers; they usually have a timing device attached to the back), here we had to earn our shirts; we wouldn't get them until we crossed the finish line. The organizers had included the same personalized touch as at the San Francisco races—the name of every competitor was displayed on the wall at the nearby Nike store. Seeing my name on that huge wall made me feel like this race was kind of a Big Deal.

As for the race course, it's hard to go wrong in D.C.; we looped past the Capitol, through the National Mall, into Virginia around Arlington National Cemetery, then back again. So many times, I could feel a lump in my throat, stemming from a mixture of pride, patriotism, and gratitude. As if the setting itself wasn't sensational enough, the many musical bands lining the course to keep competitors entertained along the way included my all-time favorite—samba drummers. It's a challenge to keep power walking when you'd rather take a dance break, but I managed to keep moving forward.

That was all well and good … and I mean really, really good … but the highlight of a Nike race is receiving the signature blue box. That the finisher shirt was also Tiffany blue added an extra layer of perfection to an already fabulous experience.

This was one of the rare occasions where I devoted a few extra days to playing tourist in a race location, checking out places in D.C. I hadn't had time to enjoy during my previous visit with an eight-year-old in tow. Just as Washington, D.C., never disappoints as a vacation destination, Nike never disappointed as a race organizer. Sadly, they brought their race series to an end a couple of years after this race, much to the consternation of its many devoted followers.

So how does the 50 States Half Marathon Club handle Washington, D.C., anyway? It's not a state but it's certainly a part of the United States. The club rules refer to it as a bonus, meaning that a D.C. race isn't required to qualify for the 50-states completion award. Had the start or finish been located in Virginia I could have ticked that state off my list but running through a state mid-race doesn't count.

Would I have traveled to D.C. solely for a bonus race? Probably not. But the tourist experience, scenic race course, and, of course, that necklace medal made it very worthwhile.

2014

Utah

Oregon

Washington

Utah

REVEL BIG COTTONWOOD, SALT LAKE CITY

Religions have long been a source of fascination for me ... not just the variety of beliefs but the rituals, the edifices, the pageantry associated with different denominations. That includes the Church of Jesus Christ of Latter-Day Saints, sometimes referred to as the Mormon Church; their temples are closed to the public, so I'd never had a chance to view the sacred spaces where their rituals are conducted.

When a work commitment required my presence in Salt Lake City, I was thrilled for an opportunity to visit the home base of the LDS Church. Bonus! There was an intriguing half marathon in town that weekend, too. Revel Big Cottonwood seemed like a race I'd enjoy; 10 downhill miles, then three more gently sloped to the finish. While many race participants hate downhills for causing their quadriceps muscles to scream in anguish, I love 'em; I feel like a bowling ball rolling down a newly waxed lane.

The most polite, well-scrubbed volunteers imaginable staffed Big Cottonwood's enormous race expo. "What shirt would you like?"

45

they inquired. "Short sleeves, long sleeves, size, style?" I was more accustomed to having shirts flung at me by harried workers trying to accommodate a large crowd; if the shirt didn't fit, well, too bad for you. Not here in Salt Lake City, where the helpers had the time and inclination to actually be helpful.

The full and half marathons started way up Cottonwood Canyon; miss the shuttle bus and you'd miss the race. My hotel at the foot of the canyon conveniently served as the bus loading spot; in fact, I'd chosen it for that very reason. Pick up time was 5:00 a.m.; that meant a 4:00 a.m. wake-up call. Race math rarely works in favor of a decent night's sleep.

After the bus drop-off, we gathered in huddled masses yearning to be warm, a difficult challenge at elevation of 7,297 feet on a pre-dawn September morning. Trembling under my heat sheet as I watched perky volunteers pour cups of coffee, I wished I'd developed a taste for that swill simply so I could warm up a bit. Hard as I'd tried, I'd never been able to tolerate coffee unless it was embellished with a shot of Bailey's and a huge dollop of whipped cream.

I also wished I'd slapped on a little makeup ... as the sun rose, I noted a high percentage of women sporting winged eyeliner plus filled in brows and lips. The approach to race readiness among the Utah ladies differed greatly from the usual California crowd. They looked great, but for me, a full face of foundation mixed with race sweat would spell dermatological disaster.

We lined up right before the starting gun was scheduled to go off, only to be informed that several buses had not yet made their way to the full marathon start line, 13 miles above us. The subsequent 30-minute delay threatened to mess with everyone's porta-potty timing, but at last we were unleashed down the canyon. Accompanied by a creek that ran alongside the course, we swept past trees arrayed in vivid reds, oranges, and golds; that dry mountain air was like an adrenaline shot that propelled me almost despite myself. Upon exiting the canyon after Mile 10 what felt like level ground was in truth a gentle decline, in contrast to the rapid descent we'd left behind; in all, the course dropped 2,856 feet in 13.1 miles.

The finish line clock showed I'd achieved a PR, or personal

record, of 2:37:12—not bad for a power walker. My first reaction upon seeing my 12:00 pace was, *"I can't believe I was so fast!"* My second reaction? *"I can't believe I missed cracking the 12-minute barrier by one stinking second per mile!"* I knew that unless I was someday dropped out of a helicopter to start a race that went straight downhill, it was unlikely I'd get close to that pace again.

Between racing and working that weekend, I carved out some time to visit Temple Square, a stunningly landscaped oasis of serenity amid the bustling downtown of Salt Lake City. My aching legs made it impossible to out-hustle the pairs of young LDS missionaries walking around helping tourists and, one assumes, low-key trawling for recruits. They kindly pointed me toward the visitor's center that housed a massive dollhouse-type structure, a replica of the Temple's interior. Later on, enjoying the autumn sunshine outside the Temple, I watched in fascination as bridal party after party streamed forth from the interior, staking out space for photos at the conclusion of their sealing ceremony (the LDS wedding rite that binds bride and groom for eternity). Any bridezilla craving a wedding day that's all about her should strike the Salt Lake Temple from her potential location list, as she's evidently doomed to fight for attention with a bevy of other brides.

Fast forward five years: I was able to assuage my curiosity about LDS temple interiors when the Oakland Temple briefly opened to outsiders post-remodel and pre-rededication. At last, I viewed firsthand the sealing rooms, baptismal font, celestial room ... the private (not secret, they stressed) places where ceremonies are held. Photos were not allowed, but no matter; those fascinating sacred spaces are etched in my mind.

Oregon

PORTLAND MARATHON (HALF)

I liked the taste of out-of-state racing I'd had in Utah; now I was hungry for more. Renowned as a walker-friendly race (meaning a very generous finish time limit) that offers swag par excellence, the Portland Marathon was the setting for my first full marathon in 2002. That positive experience compelled me to return for the half marathon a mere month after my trip to Salt Lake City. I was fortunate to participate before their organizational wheels fell off; in subsequent years this once great race has been plagued by problems: slow-moving trains stopping runners mid-race, unmarked turns sending competitors off course, even the mind-boggling gaffe of presenting awards to the wrong people. Beset by claims of mismanagement and conflicts with the city, the event changed administrators a few times; hopefully, they've now worked out the kinks.

One of the big positives with Portland is the ease of getting around. After a short flight from Oakland, the MAX light rail (with a station conveniently located at the airport) brought me quickly to the dynamic downtown. Everything was within easy walking distance—first the expo, then the hotel, and finally the start line the next morning.

With about 9,000 entrants between the full and half marathons, this race hit that sweet spot—big enough to feel like a happening, small enough that the mass of humanity didn't take an hour to cross the start line. That year's course took limited advantage of Portland's beauty; the first few miles plus the very last stretch ran through scenic parts of the city. The remainder was a slog through industrial areas, made even less enjoyable by an uncharacteristically intense October sun beating down. The post-finish line finale nearly amounted to a 14th mile: a lengthy chute where finishers could make their choices from an enormous array of snacks. Kudos to the organizers for ensuring that participants alone could access the goodies. At too many competitions, friends and family members help themselves, leaving the back-of-the-pack runners and power walkers to fight over the remaining stale plain bagels or brown bananas.

What stood out most of all about the Portland Marathon was the swag, unsurpassed by any race at least in terms of volume.

In addition to a well-designed long-sleeved tee, there was a striking medal plus a replica pendant necklace and commemorative

48

Bring an extra suitcase for Portland Marathon swag.

coin, a rose (Portland is the Rose City), a lightweight jacket, and a tree. Yes, a pine tree seedling; I dubbed mine Portlandia. I carefully protected her on the flight back home, where she was planted and fussed over through a California drought. I'm sorry to report that Portlandia died an untimely death the following year, but the medals and great race memories live forever.

49

Power Walk!

Washington

SEATTLE MARATHON (HALF)

Famous Amos cookies washed down with a Coke aren't your typical Thanksgiving dinner. But as non-traditional as my 2012 holiday meal may have been, I wouldn't have traded it for anything.

Shortly after flying to Seattle that year for a holiday celebration with my sister Jan's family, I received word of my father's rapidly failing health. Scrambling to find an available airline seat two days before Thanksgiving, I managed to get myself as close as Chicago then drove six hours through pre-holiday traffic to Michigan. And so it was that Thanksgiving dinner that year was purchased from a Traverse City gas station's mini-mart. Restaurants were not an option; I wanted to spend every possible moment with my dad, his warmth and sense of humor still very much in evidence before he passed away the following day.

I'll always be grateful for that time together. But two years later I wanted to try once more for a real Thanksgiving dinner with Jan's crew, and now I was on the lookout for opportunities to combine races with out-of-town trips. Conveniently for me, the Seattle Marathon takes place every Thanksgiving weekend. A family reunion, a holiday, and a race—perfect!

Traditional half marathon training plans don't suggest gobbling a massive Thanksgiving dinner in advance of race day, but I say why not add some fat loading to the traditional carbs? I'm positive that a few days of holiday overeating combined with hours of laughing over old family stories is an excellent pre-race abdominal workout. All too soon it was time to pack up and leave for the Westin Seattle in preparation for the next day's race.

People often comment that the runners they see look miserable. They are ... when it's 23 degrees outside.

This event marked the start of a trend I'd eventually notice in many of my race experiences: that of "this is the worst race weather we've ever had!" In this case, I was repeatedly assured that the Seattle Marathon had never been held in such a nasty chill. (Although every time I visit Seattle, I'm told that whatever massive flooding, record-setting temperatures, or other meteorological afflictions are occurring are alleged to be without precedent.) That starting temperature is the coldest I've experienced during a race. How does one dress for such sub-freezing conditions? The usual cold-weather gear, doubled, and then some. Two pair of running tights, two light-weight jackets, a short-sleeved shirt atop a long-sleeved shirt.... I was so thankful for the crowded start line area, where I sought out a spot in the middle of the pack so my fellow competitors would provide a shield from the wind as we waited for the starting gun.

The enthusiastic crowd vibrated with excitement ... or maybe that was uncontrollable shivering. By the time I'd finished, two brutal hours and 49 icy minutes later, the temperature still hadn't cracked the freezing mark. My memories of the course are few, perhaps a result of blood being diverted from my brain in an attempt to keep the rest of my body from becoming hypothermic. I recall piercing wind gusts as we traveled over sections of elevated roadway; I have a vague recollection of some picture-perfect sights around Lake Union. I spent most of the race with my eyes riveted to the ground in hopes of avoiding the little ice rinks that had developed where excess water or energy drinks had been dumped and subsequently froze. While I am an experienced ice dancer, I had no intention of busting a move, or a hip, during this race.

At the finish line, the medal turned out to be a letdown, rating an "A" for concept but a "D" for execution. I do appreciate that Seattle's most prominent architectural landmark, the Space Needle, was featured. But the overall quality was lacking, and who on earth decided that a downmarket red grosgrain ribbon was a good match with the shirt's oh-so-Seattle blue/green theme?

Once I'd defrosted, we dined at the Westin's Relish Burger Bistro. It's possible that anything would have tasted amazing after suffering through such a difficult race. But that spicy black bean burger with sea salt fries ranks among the best meals I've ever eaten, confirmed by the fact I still recall it in drooling detail years later. Thanksgiving dinner is its own kind of wonderful (assuming it's not Famous

51

Amos cookies), but a perfect bean burger and fries is a gastronomic delight without equal.

2015
Indiana
Michigan
Nevada
Arkansas
Texas

Indiana

INDIANAPOLIS HALF MARATHON

It's funny how a casual little comment can set something big in motion. In an instant, a worldview can change, or something outrageous can suddenly seem not quite so foolish.

It was one such offhand comment from my fellow power walker Kellie that partly laid the foundation for my 50-state adventure. As we devoured our free donuts following a local half marathon, Kellie mentioned, "I'm thinking of doing another half in a couple of weeks. I mean, why not? I'm already in condition!" Suddenly a lightbulb went off in my glycogen-deprived brain. I'd never thought of it that way—I'd accepted the conventional wisdom that every race would require a lengthy recovery period. Now I found that I couldn't stop thinking about what she'd said. Why not take advantage of the training I'd put in and rack up more races?

That's how I ended up at another half marathon a mere two weeks later; when I survived that in one piece, I began pounding out a 13.1-mile race every few weeks. As a newly qualified member of the Half Fanatics running club, I discovered there were thousands of people far more fanatical than I was who did this regularly, some even more often than I. What had always sounded like something for other people suddenly began to sound like something for people like me. While I still thought trying to race in every state was an unlikely prospect, the door had opened to increasing my race frequency beyond what I'd thought possible.

With four Western states now complete, I'd become hooked on the thrill of racing in different states. Other places provide surroundings, weather, and experiences that even California, with its huge menu of diverse events, can't match. But concerns about climate change plus my dislike of air travel seemed like insurmountable barriers when thinking about literally racing around the country. What choices could I make that would place the least amount of stress on myself and on the planet? The answer was to complete multiple races per trip. Even with my recently increased number of racing miles that seemed absurd. Yet people who seemed to be a lot like me—some older, many power walkers, most who wouldn't consider themselves athletes—were doing it all the time.

I'd heard intriguing things about the Detroit International Half Marathon. It received rave reviews from past participants plus it covers territory I know well from growing up in that area. If I was going to get on a plane to fly to a race, I wanted it to be something special, and I knew Detroit would be just that. But to justify the trip in my mind I wanted to find a Saturday half marathon within driving distance so I'd be good to go with a two-race weekend. Of course, good to go didn't necessarily mean good to finish; that remained to be seen.

The Indianapolis Half Marathon would be a 4.5-hour drive from Detroit— long enough to get painfully stiff sitting in a car after the race, but manageable. Despite sounding like a big-time race, there would be a medium-sized field of about a thousand competitors. Fine by me, given that Detroit would be the really big show. My main concern was surviving Indy in one piece; what a nightmare to miss out on Detroit if I managed to injure myself in Indy the day before.

Power Walk!

The trip to Indianapolis was unremarkable, save for my phone's directions from the airport to the Drury Hotel: "Follow the signs for I-70 East/I-74 West/I-465 South then take I-69 North to I-465 South to I-69 North to..." It was as though Siri had been replaced by Kristen Wiig from an episode of *Saturday Night Live*'s "The Californians."

Race morning was as chilly as expected of mid–October Indiana. The course location at Fort Harrison State Park, the former site of Fort Benjamin Harrison, meant there were plenty of old military buildings to huddle against for warmth while waiting for the start line call. Shaking like leaves being buffeted by a chill autumn breeze, the men and women chatted about the things people chat about at these shindigs:

"Where are you from?"

"What's your next race?"

"What made me think this was a good idea?"

A woman from Florida told us she'd be running another half in Wisconsin the next day, part of her plan to race in all 50 states. *Insanity!* I thought to myself. Well, yes ... but little did I know that same affliction would soon overtake me.

The course highlighted Indiana's spectacular autumn beauty. Leaves change color in my part of California, but not with the magnificence on display in the Midwest. Our route through heavily wooded areas might have been monotonous at other times, but October was on fire—with color, not actual flames as in a typical California autumn. While it was tempting to keep a fast pace in that crisp air, I resisted. *"Take it easy,"* I reminded myself, *"this is like the first half of a full marathon."* Saving energy for another 13.1 miles the next day was my top priority.

My race concluded injury-free and with some energy reserves still untapped, a good sign for the second half of my weekend. After inhaling a slice of free pizza, I began the long drive through farm country that would (hopefully) get me to the pre-race expo and packet pickup in Detroit before closing time.

Michigan

DETROIT INTERNATIONAL HALF MARATHON

Who says you can't go home again? I've made it back to Michigan on many occasions since moving to California in the 1980s. As a native of suburban Detroit with oodles of family in Ontario, I'd crossed the U.S./Canada border countless times throughout my childhood. The Detroit International Half Marathon represented a can't-miss opportunity to experience on foot a journey most people can only take by car.

My dad was what is now disparagingly termed a border baby. Grandma Mimi traveled to Michigan to give birth, then took Dad home to Ontario. The official story: Her doctor was based in Detroit. But c'mon now ... this is my dad's family we're talking about. Grandpa was an international rum runner during Prohibition; Mimi was notorious for smuggling goods to avoid paying customs duty. Her most infamous incident involved hiding a toilet seat under the broad collar of her fur coat. During my childhood this raised many questions that went unanswered: Did the toilet seat have an attached lid, and if so, how was it positioned? If she could afford a fur coat, why not pay the duty on the toilet seat? So the idea of spiriting a newborn across the border, perhaps sequestered within an oversized cloche, made perfect sense within the context of my family's history.

After fighting in World War II with the U.S. Navy, Dad wed my Canadian mum then settled down in Windsor to raise a family. When his cross-border commute to work in suburban Detroit became too much of an ordeal, they immigrated to the United States. As a result, my childhood Sundays and holidays were spent traveling the Detroit–Windsor Tunnel to visit grandparents, aunts, uncles, and cousins, the latter of whom would frequently beg me to "say something in your Yankee accent!" resulting in howls of amusement at my expense.

Several decades later I arrived in Detroit just in time to connect with my gal pal Lori then walk to the race expo. Lori had made the drive from Kalamazoo, the setting for our post-college days where we forged careers in radio. While I escaped to California following a short-lived, traumatic stint in the sales department, Lori persevered. She overcame the multitude of humiliations foisted upon women in broadcasting to rise triumphant, becoming one of Michigan's most acclaimed media personalities. Time and distance hadn't weakened our bond, because, well ... what's 35 years and 3,000 miles when together you've conquered professional headaches, romantic heartaches, and 1980s fashions?

The expo volunteers double-checked that my passport info had been prescreened to facilitate the next day's border crossing. They issued instructions to carry the passport with me anyway, in case the guards chose to pull me aside mid-race. Or, in my case, that would be passports plural—I'm a proud citizen of both the USA and the Great White North.

For the first and only time, my evening pre-race ritual expanded to include the intake of alcohol. This phenomenon may possibly be known as "the Lori Effect." While the highly enjoyable breach of training protocol didn't appear to negatively impact my race performance, I resisted the urge to incorporate booze into my routine on a regular basis. But I might have enjoyed a shot of something to warm me the next morning as we awaited the starter's gun beneath a light dusting of powdered sugar—like snow flurries.

The first two miles of the course took the chill off barely enough to avoid freezing solid when I ascended the wind-blasted entrance of the Ambassador Bridge into Canada. Adopting my best non-threatening look as the border guards sized me up, I was relieved to merely be offered high-fives; a less-fortunate (or perhaps more suspicious-looking?) runner near me was stopped for questioning. Then it was on to the bridge where I drank in the magnificent view I had missed for so many years. My sisters and I had never, despite our constant pleas, succeeded in convincing our dad to take the beauteous bridge instead of the creepy tunnel. It took several years and a major effort on my part, but I was finally crossing that danged bridge.

The good people of Windsor lined the streets to offer refreshments and shout encouragement; now it was my turn to enjoy the accents:

2. 50 States and Washington, D.C.

"Welcome to Canada!"
"Hot coffee here!"
"Grab some Timbits!"

Grabbing Timbits sounded like what my former radio bosses might have insisted I do to be promoted; it turned out Timbits are a confection from acclaimed coffee purveyor Tim Hortons. Powering down Riverside Drive, I was surprised when I began getting a little teary-eyed at the sight of the parks lining the road. My parents once overshared with me that this was where they'd gone parking back in their dating days to, ahem, "enjoy the view of Detroit." A story that had once horrified me now seemed nostalgically romantic. Oh, and that view—if they ever took a moment to look at it, it was spectacular. When seen up close the city of Detroit may suffer from a variety of well-documented problems, but from this vantage point, it was a gleaming salute to urban architecture.

Ready to run for the border at the Detroit International Half Marathon expo. Photograph by Lori Moore.

Too soon we were routed back to the States through the mile-long Detroit–Windsor Tunnel. I was relieved to see that the tunnel had been re-tiled since my younger years when I would imagine water trickling down those dirty walls in advance of the entire thing collapsing on our car at any moment. I've heard participants complain that the tunnel is hot and smelly during the race; while it's true that it wasn't as fresh as the outside air, I'd label it as tolerably dank. My one race regret was that I didn't stop and ask someone to take my photo in front of the painted flags marking the international border. It would have made a cool souvenir for a dual citizen.

The remainder of the route took us through Detroit's Corktown and Mexicantown. Mexicantown? I never knew it existed. It wasn't just the bridge that my dad avoided; he refused to spend any time in Detroit except to pass through—with car doors securely locked—on the way to and from Canada. Perhaps my life-long love for urban spaces stems in part from having been whisked so quickly past them as a child, nose pressed against the rolled-up glass of the car window.

Commemorating my first two-race weekend. Photograph by Lori Moore.

I rushed through the after-race clean-up ritual so that Lori and I could stroll to a local pub (yes, Dad, I walked through downtown Detroit and lived to tell

58

about it!). Supportive as always, Lori insisted I pose for a photo with the two medals I'd earned that weekend—a celebration of my first successful back-to-back half marathons.

As happy as I was to have two more states checked off my list, I was even more delighted, and somewhat surprised, to have survived my inaugural back-to-back weekend injury-free. I had to admit that suddenly the wacky idea of a half marathon in every state started to seem, well ... maybe not quite so wacky.

Nevada

ROCK 'N' ROLL LAS VEGAS

It was one of my most memorable birthdays; how could it not be, given that it was celebrated in Las Vegas? The fact that it was memorable—as in, I can actually remember it—is because instead of indulging in copious amounts of cocktails, I power walked 13.1 miserable miles through a cold, wet, windy Vegas night. Yeah, baby, yeah!

I'd visited Vegas twice: on a family vacation as a kid then decades later on a business trip. Nothing I'd seen had compelled me to return for a third go-round. But completing a half marathon in every state meant a trip to Nevada, and the Rock 'n' Roll Las Vegas race had a reputation as a true happening, a nighttime extravaganza that closed the Strip to vehicular traffic. I managed to persuade my sisters Jan and Mari to meet me there; with my birthday falling on the same day as the race, how could they refuse?

Thanks to that evening start time I could fly into Vegas from Oakland on race day itself. We sisters rendezvoused at Marriott's Grand Chateau, a spot close to the Strip that was a short walk away from the race village hosting the expo. Conveniently this race allowed same-day packet pickup, but here's a little-known fact: Even races that say there's no race day pickup will have bibs at the start line for people who miss the expo. Check in with the solutions desk or timing area; it's almost a sure thing your bib will be there waiting for you.

Power Walk!

Following pickup, I stayed around the race village for the pre-race entertainment: a Kid Rock concert. Admittedly he's not exactly my favorite musician, but the price was right (free, if you didn't take into account the hefty race registration fee). The village and concert location would gain notoriety two years later as the scene of the deadliest mass shooting by an individual in U.S. history. But that sad story was still in the future; on this day my thoughts were consumed by finding a curb to sit on and resting my legs until it was time to find my corral. (Yes, some of the big races herd participants into corrals, segregated by estimated finish time or pace.) I hoped I'd managed my food intake appropriately; evening races present an unusual challenge in that it's hard to know exactly how to eat that day. Too little and you'll have no energy; too much and you'll feel weighed down. I could only hope my combination of Southwest Airlines snacks and Clif Bars had struck the right balance.

Oh, those corrals. It felt like the cattle ranch from Hell: roughly 60 corrals jammed with 40,000 runners and walkers. I gave up trying to push my way up to my assigned corral; there was simply too much humanity packed into too little space. Not willing to risk bodily harm, I stayed with the group I found myself in when forward motion no longer seemed possible—although that didn't stop several overly aggressive types from shoving their way through.

Then down came the rain. A cold shower washed over the masses as we slowly inched toward the start. I'm unsure exactly how long it took my corral to cross the start line, but I do know this: I lined up when the sun was shining but started the race in the dark.

Rock 'n' Roll Las Vegas ranks very high on the list of races that provided me with the all-important visuals that distract from my discomfort. As I was newly arrived in town, Vegas's ornate tackiness was new to me as it unfolded before my astonished eyes. As promised, there were bandstands every mile or two, but the musicians were nowhere to be seen, or heard, having taken cover due to the rain. But even the foul weather couldn't dampen the enthusiasm of the couples who stopped at Mile 4 for mid-race wedding ceremonies and vow renewals. There were countless Elvii, runners in showgirl gear ... a party vibe prevailed despite the poor conditions.

60

Things went south when the race turned northeast. Neon lights gave way to unlit, sketchy neighborhoods as the weather worsened. When we returned to the Strip for the final few miles, gusting winds that had already blown over all of the race mile markers were strong enough to push me off balance more than once. The bands and spectators were long gone, a brutal way to end a most memorable race.

Once I had passed the finish line, an interminable chute led to where I could have grabbed snacks if they hadn't already been cleaned out by the faster folks who finished ahead of me. An info table volunteer handed over my race T-shirt; the woman next to me picked up her marriage license. Rock 'n' Roll Las Vegas was definitely not your typical race.

The door to the hotel room was latched from the inside when I returned, both surprising and inconvenient given an urgent need to offload my excess hydration intake. After increasingly desperate knocking, the door at last swung open to reveal a table laden with gifts and desserts, candles ablaze, as my sisters' voices rang out, "Happy Birthday!" So surprising! So kind! But I needed a bathroom *so bad*! I could hardly say, "Do you mind blowing out those candles, then re-lighting them in a minute?" I took care of the candles, ooh'ed and aah'ed for what I hoped was an appropriately appreciative (albeit painful) interval, then attended to après-race necessities.

Over the next couple of days, we enjoyed a tiny bit of gambling, a teeny bit of drinking, and a ton of junk food plus non-stop gawping at the craziness of Vegas. This is one destination where the race should happen at the start of the trip, especially for anyone hoping their time in Vegas will be memorable in the infamous "I remember nothing" sort of way.

Arkansas

CASA HALF MARATHON, PINE BLUFF

The walkways and brown lawns surrounding the redbrick campus were devoid of students that oppressively murky December morning, but what self-respecting college kid would be up at 7:00 a.m. on a Saturday? The line of racers at U of A–Pine Bluff stadium picking up bibs and T-shirts moved quickly, so I had plenty of time to engage in my pre-race ritual of standing around awkwardly before the CASA Half Marathon started. A sweet-faced volunteer checked off my name and with a "Have a great race, hon!" handed over my goodies. I've received some unusual race swag over the years ... shaving gel, laxatives, wildflower seeds... but this was the first time I'd received a cookbook. While quickly scanning *Southern Accent* (copyright 1976 by the Junior League of Pine Bluff) I swore I could feel my LDL cholesterol level rise.

After dropping the book off at my rental car, I sauntered over to the start line to eavesdrop on the other race participants.

"Oh hon, I never use GU, it makes me gassy."

A gaggle of women nodded their heads, bonding over the common runner's plight of excessive carbohydrate consumption.

"Do y'all know how long the porta-potty line is?" a gal in a Half Fanatics shirt called out. "Mah coffee went through me like shit through a goose."

"I need two Band-Aids," cried a desperate dude clad in 80s short-shorts, "this cotton shirt is gonna make mah nipples bleed."

It seemed that racers in Arkansas were every bit as good at sharing, and oversharing, as racers everywhere.

A boom from the starting gun and we were underway. The dense knot of competitors quickly thinned to a ribbon threading its way through campus then into the surrounding neighborhood. Some local residents were on their front porches that hideously muggy morning: elderly women in house dresses sweeping dirt from under white plastic chairs, dilapidated cars sprouting like rusted lawn ornaments where grass once grew. Pit bulls and German shepherds stared back from behind chain-link fences, resembling prisoners more than guards. The bleak surroundings weighed on my mood every bit as much as the humidity.

My lungs struggled to harvest oxygen from the soggy air; it was like breathing through a straw. As we entered a park filled with verdant trees, the air was no less stifling, but the new views provided a welcome distraction. Several campers emerged from tents clutching coffee cups as they observed us with mild curiosity. Are they here, I wondered, for a brief bit of respite by the lake, or are they squatters who call this place home—at least until they are caught? Perhaps I was too used to the sight of the homeless back in the Bay Area and couldn't recognize the difference between camping versus an encampment.

Our course formed an out-and-back loop through the park; after several miles, the lead runner approached from the opposite direction. I yelled out, "Way to go!" which was met with a reply of "Thank youuu! Nice job!" Never before had I heard a lead runner return the cheer of a fellow racer. Damn, but those Arkansas folks were friendly.

Leaving the park behind, we made our way back toward the empty campus ... it had been a couple of hours since we left. Perhaps the kids were still sleeping off their Friday night fun; as the parent of a college student, I hoped they were in the library studying for their upcoming final exams. Nah, probably not.

As I crossed the finish line, a medal was placed around my neck. The shiny disc indicated the race was a fundraiser for CASA, a local battered women's shelter. A good friend from Arkansas told me that Pine Bluff struggles with significant poverty and crime. Of course, domestic violence plagues all socioeconomic levels, but I could imagine that women in Pine Bluff might be especially vulnerable to finding themselves without a safety net. It's good to know that CASA is there for them.

I had nothing to complain about, but right then I felt like a sponge that had been immersed in molasses. I didn't know how I'd find enough energy to drive to Dallas, then run another half marathon the next morning. I returned to my hotel for a quick shower before I hit the road.

"How was your race, hon?" asked the desk clerk.

"Just great!" I lied, feeling the air conditioning harden the sweat on my face into a salty shell. Back in my room, I resisted the temptation to fall onto my bed, moaning. Instead, I managed a few stretching exercises then went straight to the shower. There were a lot of miles between me and Texas, and a major thunderstorm loomed between us.

Texas

Dallas Marathon (Half)

The narrowness of the bed surprised me. Atop the dresser, a book lay open as if he'd moments ago put it down; in the still, musty air, time seemed to have stood still. *Why am I taking a photo?* I thought. *I know I'll never forget the look, the feel of this place.* Then it struck me—how many others had passed here before me, how many other women could say that they, too, had been in Bill Clinton's bedroom? One last lingering look, then I turned to meet his eyes.

"Thank you, it was wonderful," I breathed.

He gave me a look that said everything he couldn't put into words ... the thrill he felt to have an actual customer that December afternoon.

"You're welcome, ma'am," drawled the Parks Department tour guide, leading me out of the former president's childhood home and into the courtyard. "Oh, and see that house right there, around the corner?" the guide continued. "That's where Mr. Clinton's friend Vince Foster lived."

I knew my Clinton history and my political gossip; Vince Foster wasn't any old friend but a rumored paramour of Hillary Clinton and the target of right-wing conspiracy theories. I was tempted to linger, to soak up whatever weird vibes there might be, but it was time to get back on the road. I was only partway to Dallas and the rain had just begun.

After completing the CASA Half Marathon that morning, I'd showered as quickly as my aching body would allow. There was time for a quick swing through the Burger King drive-thru for chicken fries and a Coke (I know, I know) before I bade farewell to Arkansas. The trip to Dallas for the next morning's race would take roughly six hours; a massive thunderstorm loomed up ahead. I'd survived horrific weather in my Michigan days, but thunderstorms of any

The room where it happened—Bill Clinton's boyhood bedroom, Hope, Arkansas.

proportion are rarely seen in California, so I was out of practice. *Please God,* I prayed, *let there be such a thing as muscle memory when it comes to driving through storms.*

The Arkansas roads that lazed from Pine Bluff toward the interstate resembled the remains of a Civil War battle. Tattered

65

Confederate flags flapped in the wind, seeming to fan the flames of the fires burning below them throughout the winter-drab landscape. *What on Earth can all of these people be burning?* I wondered. The sight of outdoor fires deliberately set then left to burn was something my wildfire-fearing Western self couldn't begin to wrap my head around.

Finally merging onto I-30, making good time was imperative as I drove ever closer toward the belly of the thunderstorm beast. After my stop at Clinton's house in Hope, churning clouds obscured the sun's last rays as I was plunged into a hellish highway scenario. Gripping the wheel as if my life depended on it (which it kind of did) I followed the singular thing I could see—the taillights in front of me. Pulling over to wait out the storm was not an option with the relentless rain obscuring the sight of exit ramps. When I arrived unscathed in Dallas hours later, I felt I'd had one of the best core workouts of my life, thanks to the many moments I'd spent clenching my abdominal muscles in abject terror.

I hoped my drive through that deluge was not for nothing, which would be the case if my race packet wasn't waiting for me at the hotel. An online stranger from the Half Fanatics running club had agreed to pick up my bib and shirt at the race expo. Some of the drive's tension drained away when the desk clerk produced my swag bag from the back office. Hurray for the Internet and the kindness of my fellow racers!

From my Omni hotel room window the next morning, I watched as the corrals filled with competitors, allowing me to make a leisurely arrival shortly before my group approached the start line. With the previous day's race lingering in the form of low energy and tired muscles, I was grateful for the distractions the half marathon course provided. In addition to various historical parts of town, we ran through Turtle Creek, one of the most elegant residential neighborhoods I'd ever seen. Stunning homes, lush landscaping, and—best of all—a large creek meandering through the middle. Those miles of prime real estate kept my mind off of my aching feet and lethargy.

Soon another medal was around my neck. Arkansas and Texas

were checked off my list, and I had survived uninjured. Two races, two states, one weekend for a second successful time; I still hadn't committed to the goal of racing in all 50 states, but if I wanted to get the most bang for my racing buck, these back-to-backs would be a crucial part of the plan.

2016
Arizona
Ohio
New Mexico

Arizona

Grand Canyon Half Marathon, Tusayan

Ah, late spring at the Grand Canyon. The vistas ... that grandeur! The, uh, snow? Yeah. Snow.

The Grand Canyon Half was my first event with Vacation Races, a company that offers competitions near national parks. Regulations prevent races from taking place within park boundaries, so this half marathon would be conducted almost exclusively on old logging and fire trails in the Kaibab National Forest. What a great excuse to visit my sister Mari, who lives a convenient 45-minute drive away—hurray for free accommodations! With it being May, the weather should have been divine, right?

Wrong.

Winter still had a chokehold on the area, perhaps not all that surprising as the contest took place at an elevation of 6,700 feet. When I arrived at the start in Tusayan, a bit south of the canyon, the sky looked threatening. It made good on that threat a short time

67

Frozen tundra in May near the Grand Canyon.

later as snow began to fall, continuing through the first few miles. Well, okay; despite my experience at the start line in Detroit, snow remained a rather novel race experience. But also? A rather cold race experience, especially when it's that cloudy and damp. I was gaining much more know-how in dressing for inclement race weather than this California girl could have imagined.

It's kind of hard to run a trail race without shoes. It's also kind of hard to keep your shoes on when traversing miles of mud, every step threatening to suction those shoes right off your feet. What might have been a fun race in a spectacular place turned into a battle to remain upright, mobile, and shod. As the temperatures crept above freezing, the snow became rain and the frozen tundra became mile after mile of thick, oozing sludge. It started to look as though someone had spiked the aid station water with booze. Competitors stumbled around like drunk college kids; some landed smack on their butts, some executed full face plants. More than once I lifted my foot only to discover that my shoe had stayed attached to the ground; lucky me to have realized this before plunging my sock down into a wet, gloppy mess. Things got so bad that when train tracks appeared, a bunch of us risked ankle sprains along the bumpy ties solely to get a break from all of that mud. I spent far less time looking up to enjoy my surroundings than staring down at the ground in an effort to ward off disaster.

It was some consolation that the finisher medal was a unique design evocative of National Park Service signs, with a gorgeous copper mounting. Instead of snack tables, Vacation Races presents their grub in individual boxes with a bento-like appeal, in addition to both of my favorite post-race refreshments: water and chocolate milk. They made for excellent energy replenishment while driving back to Mari's place. Upon arrival, I shed as much of my outer apparel as possible on the front porch to spare her sparkling home from my dirt-encrusted self, yet I still managed to make her foyer appear as though a Hopi mudhead kachina with a bad case of dandruff had stopped by.

Impressive medal from the 2016 Grand Canyon Half.

This is one race I might be tempted to do a second time, but that's because the organizers subsequently decided that June holds more promise of pleasant weather than May; based on my experience, that's a brilliant move on their part.

Ohio

Emerald City Half Marathon, Dublin

Some competitors end a race feeling like death warmed over. This is a tale of feeling like death that's been basted, buttered, then nuked in a microwave.

By 2016 I'd arrived at a point where it seemed wrong to get on a plane without bringing home a medal and T-shirt. That's why after RSVP'ing for my Aunt Jean's 85th birthday party in Windsor, Canada, my next move was to find a half marathon within driving distance. Having previously checked Michigan off my list, the best option turned out to be six hours away at Dublin, Ohio's Emerald City Half Marathon.

Joined at the party by my husband Todd, I was overwhelmed with laughter and tears, recalling so many long-forgotten memories while I renewed my relationship with countless cousins, aunts, and uncles I hadn't seen in far too many years. Before we knew it our farewell hugs were being hugged and we were headed to Ohio, where an unanticipated complication arose as we attempted to cross the border back into the United States.

"Where are you from, and how long have you been in Canada?" asked the border guard.

"California, and about four hours," replied Todd.

"Four hours?" The guard's face clouded over with obvious suspicion.

"Yes," I chimed in, "we were attending my aunt's 85th birthday party."

"You came all the way from California to Canada for a four-hour party." This was not a question; this was the start of an interrogation.

"Well, not just the party; we're going to Ohio so my husband can do a 100-kilometer bike ride while I power walk a half marathon."

2. 50 States and Washington, D.C.

I could sense the guard sizing us up. *"These pasty, past-middle-aged people are endurance athletes?"* After a few tense moments, she apparently decided that while we might not resemble athletes, we also didn't appear to be terrorists or drug smugglers; with a grunt and a smirk, she allowed us to re-enter our country.

The next morning I wondered if I'd have been better off staying in the cooler Canadian air. The temperature had already hit 70 degrees with horrendous humidity of 96 percent. Weather was one reason I had moved away from Michigan years ago; not so much to escape the harsh winters as the oppressive summer air. But there's no crying in power walking, and with all the sweating I'd be doing that day I couldn't afford to lose any additional salt or fluid.

The course began by traveling through some newly constructed neighborhoods where I wished the residents would come out from their McMansions to spray us with garden hoses. As the sun continued its climb, we passed mile after mile of cornfields where cicadas wove blankets of sound that transported me to the sweltering summer days of my non-air-conditioned youth.

Soon, other less pleasing sounds drowned out everything else— the blaring music and foghorn voice of the 3-hour pacer. I never learned her name (I suspect "Ms. Merman"), but that's quite possibly the single fact I didn't know about her by the end of the race. She was apparently determined to be a "fun" pacer, which to her meant blasting rap music while dishing up a non-stop stream of blather. Being forced to overhear conversations or another person's music for miles during a race can be annoying at any time, but on this day every bit of my tolerance was being used up merely surviving the craptacular weather.

Each time I picked up my pace in an effort to put some distance between us, the pacer increased hers as well. Now totally consumed by a desire to put her discussions of boyfriends, bodily functions, and other TMI behind me, I hustled as fast as I could—even when the course entered a park with miles of rough bridge surfaces laid over steamy, swampy wetlands. By now I was practically praying for some freak Ohio alligator to end my misery.

At last, I managed to put some space between me and the

human megaphone; my fast finish time of 2:46 under such arduous weather conditions is a testament to the power that negative factors can have on pace. Turns out it's as motivating to avoid an annoyance as it is to be propelled toward a reward. And there was indeed a reward in the form of one of my favorite race medals; it was the perfect size to show off the Celtic-themed detailing on a matte gold surface.

By race's end, the temperature had risen to 81 degrees with not even a hint of a breeze; I felt as if my Lycra clothing might melt into a toxic puddle. The race organizers deserve credit for offering free margaritas, but even that held no appeal for me. All I wanted was to drink as much water as possible on my trip back to California. Yet it was on my flight home that I learned my second hard lesson of the day, courtesy of several hours engaged in an ultimately unsuccessful battle to open the Aquafina bottle I had purchased at the Columbus airport.

Lessons learned:

1. Avoid Midwestern races in August
2. For rehydration, it's easy-to-open Dasani all the way.

New Mexico

SANTA FE THUNDER

Ah, Santa Fe. For years I'd dreamed of visiting, even once booking a trip only to cancel when life's circumstances intervened. For years afterward, Santa Fe always seemed to come in second on my list of potential vacation destinations. But a top-rated New Mexico half marathon finally gave me a reason to move Santa Fe to the top. My friend Kellie had family living in the area, providing her with a perfect excuse to join the fun.

Todd and I arranged a three-night stay but should have planned for more, as Santa Fe ended up being everything I'd hoped for and then some. Our home base, the Inn on the Alameda, was a short walk to both the downtown area and the art galleries of Canyon Road.

And we walked—a lot. Good thing, too, because there was no short-age of excellent food (although I passed on the highly touted Frito Pie).

Our peak meal experience took place at Rancho de Chimayó. The 45-minute drive from Santa Fe was oh, so very worth it. While everything we sampled was excellent, the single best thing I've eaten in my entire life was their *sopapillas*. There's no pictorial evidence of this gastronomic euphoria (I am always more interested in con-suming than photographing my food), but had a photo been taken, it surely would have shown me swooning in a fried bread induced stupor.

No kidding, they're that good.

I could wax poetic about the Georgia O'Keeffe Museum, the Farmer's Market, the architecture, the pottery ... but I was supposed to be there for a race, right?

The Santa Fe Thunder course starts at elevation 7,000 feet and goes up from there another 300 feet up ... over the first two miles. Perhaps powered by all that food, I felt particularly peppy on race day, but Kellie was not feeling the altitude love—and probably not much love toward me at that point for coming up with this idea. Once we passed the Mile 2 mark it was all downhill, 1,300 feet of down-hill, in fact, with panorama views that included the acclaimed Opera House and striking mountain vistas. I'm sure the musical entertain-ment along the way was wonderful, but this day brought about the dawning realization of a hard truth. Kellie and I suffer from negative music mojo; whenever we approach the musicians playing at a race, they take a break. We finished at the Buffalo Thunder Casino, where we prioritized energy replenishment over taking a turn at the slot machines.

I have a sole complaint when it comes to this race. It only applies to that particular year but has broad application to other races: The 2016 Santa Fe Thunder had the most egregious example of a medal that failed to capture the race spirit and/or location that I have experienced.

If a race director is putting on an event in a famous destination— in this case, Santa Fe is well known for its art community; indeed,

73

for a very specific type of artwork—and it's a place of historical and architectural significance, it's unforgivable to design a medal that could have been earned in any random location.

It's not that the medal is unattractive; it's that there's nothing about it that says "Santa Fe" except the words that spell it out. They had a good start with race shirts featuring a petroglyph design; why not incorporate that on the medal? If this had been the Gay Games

This rainbow-colored Santa Fe medal would be a great design—for a race in Kansas.

or a Pride Week race, perhaps some Kansas competition with an over-the-rainbow theme, the medal would have been fine. They managed to come up with some spectacular medals in other years, but in 2016, they blew it.

That was a minor complaint in an otherwise near-perfect experience. The course, the weather, the race organization were all magical, one of the few races I'd consider doing again if only for an excuse to eat more *sopapillas*, buy more pottery, finally make it out to Ghost Ranch ... did I mention the *sopapillas*? And yeah ... for a second chance at scoring a great medal.

2017
New York
Idaho
Montana
Colorado
Wyoming

New York

NEW YORK CITY HALF

My love for urban races very slightly exceeds my love for Tiffany—the store, the jewelry, the quintessential New York-y-ness. My obsession stems not from the viewing of a certain Audrey Hepburn film but from an old advertisement; it was a visually arresting ad featuring model Karen Elson wearing so-called Celebration Rings that triggered my fascination with the gems, the store, and the city it calls home.

That's how the New York City Half became my must-do race. Had I known then that I would eventually go for my 50-state goal, I'd have saved the best for last. But at this point, I was randomly choosing the races that appealed to me as opposed to developing a master plan. As the sister race to autumn's massive New York City Marathon, it (perhaps appropriately) has half the competitors at 25,000 and takes place a half-year earlier. It promised to be a happening, and I *love* a happening, especially one that involves Broadway, bagels, and the 5th Avenue flagship Tiffany store.

The race week weather report looked promising—promising to dump several inches of snow in a last-gasp-of-winter Snowmageddon. And snow it did, not as much as feared, but enough to send chills down the spines of Kellie and me at the prospect of running through all that white stuff. If we felt a chill just thinking about the snow, it was nothing compared to the feeling of being blasted by arctic air upon our arrival in New York.

When we decided to participate in this race the entry lottery had already closed—the NYC Half is so popular that a drawing determines who gets in. Refusing to be deterred, I discovered that by purchasing a VIP package we'd get guaranteed entries, hotel accommodations near the finish line, and a heated charter bus ride to the Central Park start line. Start spreadin' the news ... there'd be no race morning subway ride with the unwashed masses for these VIPs.

The pre-race expo at Javits Convention Center was a happening in and of itself. Despite the massive throng of people, things moved smoothly from station to station. That included the T-shirt distribution area where participants were allowed the rare and welcome opportunity to try on different sizes to find the right fit. Now properly in a New York state of mind, we were off to explore the city; thanks to gourmand Kellie having done her due diligence, we proceeded to carbo-load in style.

Race morning dawned ... and by the time the sun edged over the horizon we'd already been up and on the move for hours. The comfort of that heated bus was well worth whatever surcharge we paid for the VIP package, but it also meant rising ungodly early so the front-of-the-pack speedsters in our group would arrive at their start wave on time. (New York uses the more dignified, less bovine designation of "wave" as opposed to "corral.")

"Do you think they'll let us sit on the bus and stay warm?" Kellie asked as we arrived at the Central Park starting area. I gazed around the toasty confines of our bus.

"You have no idea," I replied, "how very much I hope so."

Moments later we stood in sub-freezing darkness surrounded by banks of snow, having been unceremoniously expelled from the buses' warm environs. Groups of runners and walkers desperately clutching silver heat sheets looked like bags of Hershey's Kisses that had been dumped all over the sidewalk. Then, materializing before us like an urban mirage, a 24-hour Apple store, that sparkling cubical oasis of central heating and abundant seating. Hundreds of us made

Ahhh, springtime in New York. Photograph by Kellie Bernardez.

our way there to avoid hypothermia for the 90 minutes that passed until the later waves were ready to roll out.

The first six miles of the course looped around Central Park; as those snowbanks sparkled in the early morning sun, we were grateful for the city's excellent work clearing the footpaths. Thoroughly warmed by now, not merely from momentum but by overwhelming happiness, I felt like the heroine of a Nora Ephron rom-com: *Snowbound in Central Park* or maybe *When Patricia Met Tiffany's*. After a brief jaunt into Harlem, we power walked through Times Square before heading down the West Side Highway. Kellie and I whooped and grinned, shouting, "We're so lucky to be doing this!" Native New Yorkers and tourists out for early morning coffee cheered us on; the surroundings were a non-stop source of entertainment, and when we arrived at the Wall Street finish line, it felt like we'd traveled three miles instead of 13.1.

Once we thawed out at the Millennium Hilton, it was time to resume cruising New York for food and fun. There was pizza. There was deli. There were bagels. There were black and white cookies. There was Broadway (*War Paint*, starring the acclaimed Miss Patti LuPone). I dragged Kellie along on the NBC Studios tour—my third time, and if I can ever manage a fourth, I'll do it. And need I say … there was an excursion to Tiffany & Co.

I'm not capable of winning races, and that's okay. I know my strengths and weaknesses, and as a power walker, speed isn't my strong suit compared to a runner. But I *am* capable of some first-place finishes. My county fair's table setting contest offers a category for settings based on books and movies. I'm as proud of my first-place ribbon for this setting inspired by—what else?—*Breakfast at Tiffany's* as I am of any race medal I've earned.

Idaho

Coeur d'Alene Marathon (Half)

Competitors are rarely offered a sneak peek at race medals—my guess is it happens when the race director feels confident the design will encourage fence-sitters to register so they can score that sweet bling. I don't always choose races based on the medal, but when checking out potential Idaho events, I noticed that many races utilized a potato in their design. Now when it comes to eating, there is no doubt that I love me some taters. But I find their aesthetics lacking, earning them a solid last place on my list of desirable medal designs along with that perennial non-favorite, the running shoe sole print.

So the Coeur d'Alene Marathon had one big thing going for it—no history of potato medals. Another point in its favor? It's an appealing vacation destination. A scenic race course, no potato medals … that's all the inspiration Kellie and I needed to sign up.

I won first place ... just not in a race. Photograph by Isabel Gomez.

Although on a map it appeared somewhat isolated, Coeur d'Alene was actually relatively accessible—a direct flight from Oakland to Spokane, then under an hour by car. This turned out to be one of those logistical dream races: both the expo (where we picked up race swag including race-themed pint glasses) and the start line were a short walk from our hotel, the fabulous Coeur d'Alene Resort.

The warm, cloudless race day weather couldn't have been more perfect for cruising around the course that ringed the sparkling, true-blue lake. (Although in all honesty, after several miles, city-loving me found that the view became a little monotonous.) The main challenge on this course was the road camber; there was a noticeable slant to the pavement that required lots of shifting around to ensure we didn't do the entire 13.1 miles with one hip higher than the other. Power walking on an angled roadway for several miles is almost a guaranteed way to end up with a sore back, hips, or legs.

This day was a milestone for both me and for the race itself. It was celebrating its 40th edition; this was my 50th lifetime half marathon. While we were chugging around the lake, Kellie asked the question that had been nagging at the back of my mind.

"So now that you've hit 50 halfs, are you going to go for all 50 states?"

This was state #14 for me. Fifty states still seemed light-years, and lots of East Coast plane trips, away.

"No," I told Kellie, "I think 35 states will probably be my tipping point. If I reach that number, it seems like it would be worth it to finish the rest off. But I can't see that happening."

I marked the occasion by making a goofy "50" sign with my fingers at the finish line. The race marked the occasion by giving us a goofy medal that consisted of a stylized "40." While I do wish there had been something more Idaho-y about it, at least it wasn't a spud in running shoes. The race swag also included a cotton hoodie sweatshirt. That's not my favorite garment, but it was put to good use as an extra layer at a freezing race that autumn where I was able to drop it guilt-free after the first few miles. Organizers typically scoop up any clothing dropped by participants along a race course for donation to local charities.

Our remaining time in Coeur d'Alene was spent checking out the cute downtown where we were bombarded by the omnipresent huckleberry. Huckleberry was available in pretty much every form imaginable, most spectacularly the locally-made ice cream. Smart move on their part; those famous Idaho potatoes have many splendid uses but as either an ice cream flavor or a medal design—I'll pass.

Opposite: **Commemorating 50 lifetime half marathons. Photograph by Kellie Bernardez.**

Montana

Missoula Marathon (Half)

So I'm at this *walima* (that's a Muslim wedding banquet), completely immersed in the sensational Pakistani food, the rhythms of the *bhangra* dancing ... but my phone won't stop buzzing. I give in, discovering that the source of my annoyance is Alaska Airlines. My next day's flight to Missoula has been canceled, but they've booked me on an alternative itinerary that will get me to Montana a few hours later than planned. That delay means I'll be too late for packet pickup at the Missoula Marathon race expo.

Hmph. That could have spelled race day disaster, but the organizers had provided an option I've never encountered at other competitions. After the close of bib pickup on Saturday afternoon, volunteers would bring race packets to the airport for late arrivals. Now *that* is amazing service. One quick email to the race officials and my situation was resolved, my panic momentarily quelled.

But there's another reliable source of panic on race trips—flying. The scary mini-plane I was re-routed on from Portland to Missoula tumbled around in turbulence significant enough to elicit screams from several passengers, although not from me as I'm more the "suffer in silence, white-knuckle" type. Despite the drama, we landed safely, and I had time before the race packets arrived to make a pilgrimage of sorts. A few years earlier my brother-in-law, Mike Flynn, was the co-pilot of an air tanker flight that departed Missoula en route to a wildland fire in New Mexico. The plane encountered bad weather in Utah; the crew perished on a mountainside. A memorial dedicated to the three-man crew was constructed just outside the Missoula airport terminal, and this was a perfect opportunity to pay my respects.

Once my race bib was in hand it was time to find my hotel, but not until I had engaged in battle with my rental car. This was not my first nor would it be my last encounter with a keyless ignition system, but it's the only one that's driven me to the brink of dehydration. After 10 sweaty minutes of hapless flailing around inside the

140-degree interior, the wretched thing finally booted up. Arriving at last at the overpriced Quality Inn, I drew back the curtains to reveal a view of what appeared to be an auto repair joint; at least the room was clean, quiet, and significantly cooler than 140 degrees.

The next morning, I needed 14 of the 15 extra minutes I had factored into my schedule to start that danged car for the drive to the University of Montana campus, where participants boarded buses that ferried us to the race's start area. We arrived at the staging area with plenty of time to spare, so it seemed like a good opportunity to visit the porta-potties.

I like rules. I make lots of random rules for myself. One of those rules is: Don't look around, or, God forbid, down, in a porta-potty. This was an easy rule to follow in Missoula as it was still dark outside, turning the potty's interior pitch black. So I did my thing, and as I stood up, a sickening realization came over me ... this potty had a lid, and that lid had been down. I mean, come on, I didn't sit down directly on the thing. Everyone hovers, right? So how was I to know the lid was down? It was dark and I don't look!

I quickly considered my options. It was tempting to skulk away under cover of darkness, leaving some poor bastard to suffer for my mistake. But I am my mother's daughter, and I could not simply walk away. (Although if I were truly my mother's daughter I would not have gone near a porta-potty in the first place, instead suffering silently in tragically Victorian fashion, resulting in my eventual hospitalization.) So I grabbed some toilet paper and tried to clean up as best I could while simultaneously attempting not to retch. I was successful on both counts, and darkness concealed my shame as I beat a hasty retreat from the potty.

As dawn finally broke over Missoula, the race began to the accompaniment of start-line fireworks. As dazzling as they were, they were no match for the idyllic course. Winding roads took us past rivers and countryside; although it's a mostly flat course, it felt like a gentle downhill at a non-quad-killing angle. The fireworks were not our only surprise; around Mile 3 this tuxedo-clad gentleman played a grand piano set amid a bucolic pasture—possibly the most amazing and certainly the most incongruous sight I've ever encountered

In Missoula, the best-ever random race sighting. Photograph by Kellie Bernardez.

during a race. This was no mid-race hallucination; I later learned that pianist Gary Bowman is a very real fixture along the race course year after year.

The half marathon course was so breathtakingly distracting that it was a surprise when I found myself at the finish line in historic downtown Missoula. I made a quick swing through the after-party before trudging another mile or so back to my car ... easy to find thanks to the huge "M" painted high on a nearby mountain. Relieved to get off my feet, anticipating a nice, long shower, I realized I'd forgotten to pick up my T-shirt.

I was tired. Streets throughout the town were closed due to the race. Did I want the shirt so much that I'd attempt to navigate an unfamiliar place then walk even more? Yes. Yes, I did. And it was worth it; the shirt and medal design captured the Montana spirit, so I'm glad I made the effort (including another 10 minutes to get the car started). It capped off an all-around spectacular event; even flying home through that Montana mountain turbulence on Allegiant Air couldn't spoil the afterglow.

Colorado

Rocky Mountain Half Marathon, Estes Park

If I listed the many ways my body isn't cut out for endurance sports, well ... it'd be a long, long list. I'm much more endomorph than ectomorph (that means more fluffy than skinny). You know those gloriously fine-boned distance runners with calf muscles that look like cantaloupes? That's not me. No fancy Vo2 Max tests are required to tell me that my heart and lungs didn't earmark me as someone destined for Olympic glory. One of my legs is longer than the other, then there are my highly arched, rigid feet ... but there's one thing I can't complain about: my ability to adjust quickly to high altitudes.

That comes in handy when I travel from my 350-feet-above-sea-level surroundings to places like Pike's Peak in Colorado or Maui's Haleakala. While others vomit or clutch their throbbing heads, I feel fine. It also helps when traveling to races in high places, such as Vacation Races' Rocky Mountain Half Marathon, which tops out at elevation 7,934 feet. Many people benefit from spending a few days at elevation before undertaking a race so they can adjust to the thinner air. But for me, arriving in town the day prior works out great.

That meant flying into Denver, where my husband Todd barely managed to conceal his embarrassment at my obvious enjoyment of the terminal train recordings. Hey, it's not just me who loves 'em; the Western-themed tunes are so popular they can be downloaded as phone ringtones. Kudos go to DIA for establishing the proper mood right from the start of a visitor's arrival in the Wild West. A two-hour drive brought us to the Estes Park Resort, a journey for which we later received a most impressive bill for tolls and non-payment fees we'd unknowingly racked up. Rental car pro tip: Always get the transponder.

This being a Vacation Races event, it featured their typical excellent organization. The expo was low-key and friendly, leaving us plenty of time to relax at the lodge-style resort; the restaurant was so good that I was happy to consume my pre-race meal there rather than exploring the town. It also offered a view of glittering Lake Estes, a highlight in the early stages of the next day's race route.

About that route ... well, it was the mountains of Colorado. It was scenic, dramatic, awe-inspiring. With snow-capped peaks as a backdrop, we made a quick loop around the lake then powered up and down the course as the sun gradually turned up the temperature from early morning cool to midday warmth. All around me, runners and walkers gushed over our surroundings.

Other people: "Oh my gosh! Check out these sensational vistas!"

Me: "Oh look, another mountain. That's nice."

Yeah, yeah, me and my love of urban races ... but even I had to admit there was one thing threatening to take my breath away—not the elevation, but the scenery.

The best part was that I had skipped reading the course description in the newsletter that Vacation Races provides to every participant. I rarely preview the descriptions, because I like some element of surprise during a race. Some day the surprise will be me getting lost, but on this day my lack of knowledge worked in my favor. I'd heard the course had a tough elevation change in the latter miles. Approaching Mile 9, I psyched myself for the big turn upward ... but

Things only went up—way up—from here on the Colorado course. Photograph by Todd Nelson.

it didn't arrive. Mile 10 came and went ... nothing yet. Mile 11... nada. I crossed the finish line feeling more than a little impressed with myself.

"I didn't even notice the hills in those last few miles," I remarked to some nearby fellow finishers.

"Oh, they changed the course this year," a woman laughed. "Now the hills are near the start."

Okay, I admit to feeling a little stupid for being so cocky, but mostly I was relieved that the feared uphill climb turned out to be nothing to fear after all.

Power Walk!

Before flying out of Denver that evening we caught the start of the Colorado Classic bike race in RiNo, Denver's vibrant art district. I'd love to go back there someday to check out the brewpubs and galleries. But on that day, we had more toll roads to travel then a flight to catch for the trip back to sea level.

Wyoming

Jackson Hole Marathon/Hole Half

We broke up a couple of years ago, Tom Collins and me. I dumped my friend Margarita along with our pals Bloody Mary and Harvey Wallbanger.

It was the trip to Wyoming for the Hole Half Marathon that marked my final hook-up with any kind of alcohol. I'd never been much of a drinker yet had my own version of a drinking problem: Two or three sips and it was goodbye inhibitions—but only where food was concerned. My version of the Morning After was awakening to a hangover of the literal kind, a bloated belly hanging over my pajama waistband. I can't count the number of times I've heard, "You're going to be so skinny with all of these races!" Well, not when a race burns off perhaps a thousand calories but is followed by a 3,000-calorie booze-inspired food fest.

On this September sojourn to Wyoming, Todd planned to enjoy one of his daylong bike rides while I was doing my power walk thing. The four-hour drive to Jackson from Salt Lake City's airport provided a preview of stunning peaks and rushing rivers; I wouldn't have been surprised to come across Brad Pitt doing a little fly fishing. In Jackson, we found the (very) small race expo, picked up Todd's rental bike, then drove a few more miles to our Teton Village hotel.

The next day's crystal-clear weather could not have been more perfect for a race or a ride. After rising at o-dark-thirty to catch a shuttle bus in the Village to the race start, I once again gave thanks that elevation isn't an issue for me; some people were suffering from the thin air at 6,300 feet when merely standing still waiting for the bus.

Stunning Jackson Hole finish line surroundings.

It was possibly some relief for my fellow competitors that the course itself was relatively flat. While the views of the surrounding mountains were jaw-dropping, the valley floor we crisscrossed via various parks and neighborhoods is the reason for that "hole" in Jackson Hole, the term early trappers employed to describe the basin. That gave this course a different vibe than my Colorado and Montana experiences; instead of being among the mountains, this time I could appreciate their majesty from a distance.

With about 400 competitors the race had a relaxed feeling fully in evidence at the finish line on the grassy Teton Village Commons.

After crossing the line, I found a shady spot from which to applaud the other finishers while taking a photo of my latest medal, very "Georgia O'Keeffe travels to the Tetons."

The next few days were devoted to touring the town of Jackson and hitting up Yellowstone National Park plus eating and drinking to our hearts' content (and undoubtedly our future clogged arteries). There were excellent brewpubs, outstanding cafés, and a Mexican place on Jackson's main drag where we parked ourselves in front of the bartender. While enjoying a margarita (or two), a sweet little basket of chips caught my eye from the other end of the bar.

You know how the story ends.

Soon three empty baskets stared back at me, a picture of poor choices framed by telltale remnants of salsa and guacamole. Yet they proved to be merely a foundation for the burrito-based decadence to follow. Even returning to Teton Village provided no respite, as its fruity libations rendered me powerless to

Jackson Hole featured an all-time favorite medal.

resist culinary temptation. After that, I made my decision to stay off the hooch for good.

It wasn't easy, but somehow I managed to find clothes that still fit for our drive back to Salt Lake City. We ran out of time for a side trip to Preston, Idaho, the setting for one of the greatest films ever made, *Napoleon Dynamite.* I was sad to learn they no longer host their Napoleon Dynamite Festival, which featured a tetherball tournament, tater tot eating contest, and moon boot dance. Should anyone ever organize a race where competitors are required to run (or dance) like Napoleon, I'll be the first in line to register. Think of all the calories that 13.1 miles of those moves would burn off. Dietary restraint be damned—I could devour all the tots I wanted, even a danged quesadilla or two.

2018

Louisiana
Alaska
Wisconsin
Illinois
Missouri
Iowa
Oklahoma

Louisiana

ROCK 'N' ROLL NEW ORLEANS

"Is that ... crime scene tape?"

Welcome to New Orleans, ladies and gentlemen ... *laissez les bons temps roulet*!

Home for the next few days, the New Orleans Marriott was inaccessible thanks to mass quantities of yellow tape barricading the entrance. I looked around for cameras; perhaps a movie or TV show was being filmed? There were none to be seen. Kellie and I never did find out what happened; hotel staff responded to our queries with pleas of ignorance. Luckily that was our singular brush with crime while in NOLA for the Rock 'n' Roll Half Marathon and 5K.

Yes, two races. Why settle for one shirt and medal when you can score two shirts and three medals? The Rock 'n' Roll race series knows that many racers are sucked in by lots of swag. Multiple races mean not only a medal for each race but an extra medal for the so-called Remix Challenge. It probably costs less than a buck to manufacture a medal, but I'm guessing it creates lots of dough from additional race registrations.

Dough. Did someone say dough?

Beignets ... poboys ... we were in New Orleans not solely for swag but also for the outstanding food. Normally I steer clear of any place labeled a gastropub; it sounds more like food poisoning than a place to dine. But that's where the poboys were so that's where we went, to assuage Kellie's craving. For me, the name poboy ranks right up there with gastropub as an appetite suppressant, but she claims they tasted great. I took her word for it.

Beignets were another story; I was eager to give them a go, and Café du Monde did not disappoint. Running author Rachel Toor has written that she allows herself to eat anything she wants after a race; I allow myself to eat anything I want before *and* after a race (but not during.... I do have some self-control. Sheesh.). It turns out beignets aren't merely physically filling but also sensorially fulfilling and I utterly enjoyed those hot, puffed pockets of fried dough drowning in powdered sugar. Should I be ashamed or proud of the fact that I often return home from races not just the same weight as when I left but sometimes a little heavier?

Medals should have been awarded for the act of walking through the Morial Convention Center for the packet pickup expo; at 11 freaking blocks long, it was an event in itself. At first glance the race

Kellie races the expo mannequins in New Orleans.

T-shirts confused me; why were a speaker and a guitar being placed into what appeared to be laundry baskets? Then I realized the laundry baskets were meant to be streetcars. I'm not sure of the rationale behind a speaker and a guitar being placed into streetcars, either, but at least streetcars were related to the race locale.

93

Power Walk!

The 5K race through the French Quarter on Saturday was a nice tune-up for the main event the next day. The half marathon course took us up and down St. Charles Avenue, past gracious homes in the Garden District plus the campuses of Loyola and Tulane universities. Strands of Mardi Gras beads dripped from trees like glitzy moss, colorful remnants of prior revelry. Not all of the partying was past tense; at times we were power walking through noxious clouds of weed. New York may be the city that never sleeps, but New Orleans is the city that never sobers up.

Thanks to a bad hotel mattress Kellie's back was acting up. A couple of miles into the race she suddenly veered off.

"Don't wait for me, I'll catch up!" she shouted, ducking into a drugstore.

Thus commenced a race-manners dilemma: Should I continue or stop? In a race field of thousands, what were the odds she'd find me? I settled on a slow shuffle until a few minutes later when Kellie emerged alongside me, Advil in hand. Swiping a bag of ice from an aid station, she jammed it down the back of her pants, giving her a super attractive "Hunchback of NOLA" look. Within a few miles, the ice had melted.

"It's not showing, is it?"

"Um ... yeah," I told her. "There's a massive wet area on your butt."

Thankfully the warm, dry weather rendered any potential humiliation short-lived.

This race weekend featured yet another missed opportunity to meet my hero, marathon legend Kathrine Switzer. I was denied the chance to high-five Ms. Switzer at the Victoria Marathon a few years earlier when some guy cut in front of me right at the line where she stood greeting finishers. Now spying her in Lafayette Park post-race, I thought *at last, here's my chance to meet my idol!* But when I sidled up to her group I noticed the women all wore "261" logos; I backed off, fearful of invading a private gathering. I later learned that Switzer had created a running program for women called 261 Fearless (a reference to her first Boston Marathon bib number); this was their group meet-up. I should have gone for it—she probably would have

94

Graceful trees frame the NOLA race course. Photograph by Kellie Bernardez.

been very courteous—but I'll never know because I chickened out; to this day my life remains sadly Switzer-less.

With our racing done, we had one final day in New Orleans to enjoy some jazz in the French Quarter, check out the World War II Museum (well worth it), and, yes ... eat. Rock 'n' Roll New Orleans can be summed up by the numbers—three new medals, two new T-shirts, and two new pounds of flab.

Je ne regrette rien.

Alaska

Juneau Marathon (Half)

"You're going by yourself? For a weekend? But it's so far away!"

Eh ... not so much. From the Bay Area, Alaska's a quicker trip than some places in the lower 48—a two-hour flight to Seattle, two and a half more to Juneau. Still, my friends were surprised that I was going up there for a race. Quite frankly, so was I. Despite earlier estimating that having 35 states in the bag would be my tipping point for deciding to pursue all 50, it turned out my magic number was about half that, 18. Sometime in the months after my race in New Orleans I committed to reaching that far-off destination, thinking the New England states might end up being a future retirement road trip that Todd and I would someday take. So here I was, booking my flight to Juneau.

I'd previously visited Alaska's state capital on a cruise, seeing most of what the town had to offer; spending a single night on this return visit would have been enough, but even *I* thought that seemed a little ridiculous, so I scheduled a full weekend. Either Uber hadn't yet colonized Juneau or all the drivers were otherwise engaged, but catching a cab at the airport when I arrived was no problem. Twenty-five dollars plus several bad cabbie jokes later, I checked in at the Four Points by Sheraton. What are the odds that both times I've traveled to Alaska it's been in the midst of a record heatwave? The window in my room was wide open, a portable fan running full blast—Juneau's version of air conditioning to combat temperatures in the mid–80s.

Bib and shirt pickup was about a block away; even though I arrived well before the scheduled start, the volunteers were happy to hand over my swag. The shirt was a nice tech fabric but limited to what is laughably termed unisex sizing. Unisex is code for man-cut shirts offered in sizes from not-that-small to hella-huge. Hey, race directors—since the majority of race participants are women, why not make women's shirts the default? Men wouldn't look any worse in a woman's fitted shirt than I do drowning in a big, boxy man-shirt.

It felt deliciously decadent to awaken at a relatively late time the next morning—Hawaii and Alaska are the two states where the time zone change works in a Californian's favor. A leisurely five-minute stroll brought me to Juneau's cruise ship dock; from there the race provided a shuttle bus to the start on Douglas Island, but, oddly, no shuttle back. The dock teemed with disembarked cruisers in search of transportation to area excursions. Working my way through the crowd like a salmon swimming upstream through schools of confused senior citizen fish, I finally located the race group. Consisting of crew members from several ships, this bunch exhibited the energy and enthusiasm of sailors who had moments ago been released for some hard-earned shore leave.

Our short, raucous ride to the island brought us to Savikko Park. The good news was that the park had actual bathroom facilities; the bad news was that the architect had not considered stall doors to be a key design feature. With no gear check to be found, I dropped my bag behind a random race sign near the totem pole hoping it would still be there when I finished (it was).

Mingling among the small field of athletes as the clock ticked down to the start resulted in a fortuitous eavesdropping experience; unbeknownst to me, participants were required to check in with a woman near the start line. This race didn't use timing chips, those little devices attached to the back of race bibs that track how long we're out on the course. As a result, its old-school manual timing required making our presence known to a clipboard-carrying official. Not receiving an official time would have been heartbreaking after traveling so far to get there.

Then we were off. The view was pleasant enough, with vistas that featured all the evergreen trees you could possibly want along the rolling out-and-back course on the Douglas Highway. Unfortunately, the road wasn't closed to traffic; plenty of trucks and cars swooshed past as racers hugged the side of the highway. As I returned to the

The start/finish line in Juneau was visible from quite a distance thanks to this totem pole.

park for the finale, the sofa I'd seen randomly plonked near the finish line called out to me, but I resisted the urge to succumb.

The finisher medal was nice in the old-school medal tradition; I liked the non-gargantuan size plus the Alaska landscape design. Although this race didn't do age-group awards, the results showed I placed third in the female Grandmaster category. The surge of pride I felt at placing in my age group mixed with angst over my new label. Holy hell—grandmaster? Soon enough, though, I fully embraced it; should I ever become a rapper, I'm totally going to incorporate Grandmaster into my rap name.

I'd loved to have sampled the highly recommended salmon sandwich, but the bus back to town came by on the half-hour; it was due in a few minutes and I wasn't quite sure where to catch it. I took off at a speed roughly equal to my race pace, locating the stop right as the bus pulled up. Two sweat-soaked dollar bills bought me a ride back to my hotel. I enjoyed an excellent veggie burger and fries at the hotel's sports bar, and my waiter earned a spot in the pantheon of legendary servers by placing an entire pitcher of Coke on the table. I may not have slept much that night but it was well worth it.

Leaving the hotel later for some highly caffeinated sightsee- ing, I spotted a guy in the elevator wearing a Mainly Marathons hat. That was a race series I'd considered doing, so it seemed like a good opportunity to learn a little more from someone in the know. I put on my best pretend-extrovert smile.

"Oh, did you do the Mainly Marathons series?"

"Yeah. I'm not talking right now."

He turned away, planting his face in the corner of the elevator until the door opened, then ejecting himself at high speed into the lobby. You have a nice day, too, sir. My Mainly Marathons research would have to wait until the Des Moines Marathon a few months later, where yet another socially awkward experience awaited.

I hauled myself up and down the hills of Juneau to the extent my weary legs would allow, visiting the intricately detailed Rus- sian Orthodox church and the homey Governor's Mansion (Tina Fey quips to the contrary, you can *not* see Russia from there) and passing umpteen stores hawking tanzanite jewelry. Much as I adore that purple-blue gemstone, I was content to stick with my finish line bling.

Wisconsin

Brewers Mini-Marathon, Milwaukee

"Someone's in my room!"

The quiet of the Marriott Courtyard hotel was shattered by a booming voice. A man, angry and upset, repeatedly rattled the hotel room door.

"Who's in here? This is my room!"

The person in his room? That would be me (or, for you pedants out there, that would be I). But it wasn't his room, it was mine, the room I'd been assigned upon arrival a short time earlier. Thankfully I'd remembered to flip the door latch that was now the one thing guarding me against my would-be intruder.

"This is my room," I called out. "Go talk to the front desk."

"I was assigned this room!" he bellowed, relentless in his attempt to make the door yield to his pummeling.

When the man finally realized that (1) I wasn't going to budge and (2) the door wasn't going to budge either, he retreated. Shaken by the attempted invasion, I resumed my pre-race preparations—until a few minutes later, when the door popped partly open again. This time, a woman's voice rang out.

"Who's in here?" she called sharply. "Open the door."

Again I explained I'd been given the room at check-in.

"I'm a front desk clerk," she replied, "and this man was assigned to this room."

Exhausted from a long day that suddenly seemed to be getting ever so much longer, I declined the command to open the door, instead suggesting that the clerk go back to the lobby and talk to the person who checked me in. At last, the pair departed; a call to the front desk revealed that the desk clerk who originally assisted me had neglected to remove my room from the availability list.

Welcome to Milwaukee, Marriott style. I was wiped out from a long flight plus what should have been a two-hour drive from Chicago. Those two hours had become four thanks to Friday afternoon rush hour, massive amounts of construction, and a series of confounding tollbooths that featured varying layouts and payment methods.

The situation and my mood improved the next morning. The Brewers Mini-Marathon starts and ends at Miller Park, an easy 15-minute drive from the hotel with the abundant parking you'd expect from a major league baseball stadium. I picked up my bib and T-shirt plus a bonus Brewers bobblehead doll that I couldn't envision being able to fit into my tightly packed suitcase. The air was as crisp as an Autumn Glory apple; a suffocating weather front had mercifully blown out of town the day before.

The course included sites such as the Harley Davidson Museum, Marquette University, and Miller Valley, home of the eponymous

A clue as to the post-race refreshments.

101

brewery. These particular destinations may explain why many parts of Milwaukee reeked of stale beer vomit. The flat course then worked its way through a lush, non-olfactory-offensive green space area before returning to Miller Park for the grand finale—a triumphant run into the stadium. I seek out races that incorporate venues such as stadiums; it adds a bit of pizazz to the route even though the stands are mostly empty. In we went, circling the warning track ... and then right back out. Hey, wait a second—what happened to the big stadium finish, my moment of glory? Once again, my tendency not to look closely at race routes resulted in an element of surprise. This race didn't end inside the stadium; instead, we departed the field via a dank interior tunnel then crossed a finish line in the parking lot. Well ... it was fun to run around inside the stadium if not exactly the epic finish line moment I had envisioned.

Not surprisingly there was beer at the finish; not surprisingly it was Miller Beer; not surprisingly I didn't drink the beer. I didn't even pose for a photo with Bernie Brewer, the friendly yet frighteningly oversized mascot who lurked in the parking lot accosting finishers for selfies. I was due back to Chicago for another race the next day; one breaking-and-entering-free shower later, it was time for more frolicking fun on I-94.

Illinois

Chicago Half Marathon

Packet pickup instructions for most races ask you to bring a photo ID. But I've never, ever been asked to *show* that ID, except at the Chicago Half Marathon—which was, naturally, the one time I didn't have it.

My wallet was lodged in the deep, dark recesses of my rental car, having been flung in frustration after yet another encounter with a perplexingly malfunctional Illinois Tollway booth. I'd finally given up—I peeled off, toll unpaid, wallet out of sight and out of mind. Now the race expo volunteer was refusing to hand over my bib. Okay, I suppose I could have been some random petty criminal trying to

I'd see much more of the stunning Chicago skyline the next day.

score a free shirt who coincidentally happened to know the name of someone registered for the race. Whatever. Heaving what I hoped was a dramatic sigh of resignation, I trudged what felt like 13.1 miles back to the car, then returned for my bib, beautiful long-sleeved T-shirt, and cheesy skyline photo op.

Since I'd already completed a half marathon in Milwaukee that morning, I was beyond ready to relax. But there wasn't time for that yet. First, the car had to be dropped at Midway airport before I could Uber to my hotel. Shades of New Orleans—the driver couldn't get close to the La Quinta entrance due to the fire trucks parked everywhere. But this was no catastrophe scene—the desk clerk excitedly informed me that the television show *Chicago Fire* would be filming an episode starting the next day. That meant no breakfast service in the lobby; instead, hotel guests were sent to a café down the street.

It was the sole restaurant around and I was (as usual) hungry, so I decided to check out the café's dinner offerings. Upon entering I thought perhaps a TV show was being filmed there as well; a remake

103

of *All in the Family* or maybe *The Jeffersons*. The décor, menus, clientele ... even the dead flies lining the sills of the unwashed windows dated from the '70s. My meal of bland spaghetti plus iceberg lettuce salad was so unironically retro I'm surprised my hair didn't spontaneously flip back into Farrah Fawcett wings.

At an urban race, I can usually find other folks to join on the walk to the start line, but on race morning the lobby and surrounding streets were empty in the pre-dawn darkness. Chicago's South Side doesn't have the best reputation for safety; I felt a little less anxious once I connected with a friendly couple from Colombia who'd traveled to the United States for a race vacation. I thought the area, with its old brick homes and majestic trees, looked stately and not the least bit sketchy. But then I'm the gal who thought she was driving through a decent part of Oakland when a man was gunned down in front of her, so perhaps my judgment of these things is lacking.

The Chicago Half delivered on its promise to be fast, flat, and scenic. Lake Shore Drive was shut down for the race; the course offered mile after mile of sensational Chicago skyline views. The weather was early-autumn perfect, something I especially appreciated since my energy stores were greatly depleted after the previous day's race. But upon reaching the finish line, I needed every bit of strength I could muster simply to remain upright. It wasn't exhaustion that nearly did me in but the medal that was placed around my neck. Measuring four feet long and weighing 57 pounds (I may be exaggerating a little bit) the jaw-dropping medal is the embodiment of too much of a good thing. While I love medals that highlight iconic landmarks of the host city, this plate-sized medallion nearly gave me a permanent dowager's hump.

The half-hour walk back to the hotel seemed to last for days thanks to that millstone of a medal I bore around my neck. Opting not to step back into the '70s time machine for lunch, I Uber-ed elsewhere. Should I have been concerned when the driver dropped me off with a maternal sounding "Be careful"? The food gave me the energy boost I needed to walk another mile, this time to President Obama's Chicago home. Michelle was in town that weekend (I feel I can call her Michelle; now that I've been to her house and read her autobiography, we're pretty much besties). I didn't see her but certainly noticed the fleet of massive black Secret Service SUVs with Maryland license plates parked everywhere. Sitting across the street taking photos, I probably lingered just long enough to pique the interest of agents who undoubtedly have video surveillance footage of me on file with the FBI.

How fortunate was I to have one additional day to spend in Chicago, which I used to reenact as much of *Ferris Bueller's Day Off* as possible—viewing Calder's *Flamingo* statue, spending hours at the sprawling, magnificent Art Institute of Chicago—nearly everything Ferris and his friends got up to, short of putting a Ferrari on blocks to run the odometer backward.

Missouri

Kansas City Marathon (Half)

It's a wonderful thing when race logistics work out perfectly. The Kansas City Marathon should win an award for providing participants with a dream set-up that makes racing so easy.

Following my direct flight from Oakland (no scary mini-planes or dicey connections), Kellie and I reunited at the airport; it was our first time seeing each other since she moved to Montana over the summer. Meeting up for races around the country would turn out to be a perfect way to stay connected despite the miles between us. At the race's host hotel, the Westin Kansas City at Crown Center, we discovered that the race expo was, oh, maybe a three-minute walk away. Union Station, directly across the street from the Westin, is a dazzling historic train station repurposed into an event center that would have merited a visit on its own.

We had lots of swag to pick up—not merely this race's bib and pullover hoodie (in lieu of the typical shirt) but also a long-sleeved shirt for the I-35 Challenge. Completing the Kansas City and Des Moines races in one weekend meant an extra medal and shirt. Heck, yeah! The Kansas City Marathon is also a featured race for the Half Fanatics running club. The first of their perks was a custom beer glass I received at their expo booth. Boom—a souvenir for my husband checked off the to-do list, a big upgrade from the energy bar samples he usually has to settle for.

Then it was time to eat. (FYI—it's always time to eat.) Kellie steered us to an Italian place located in a former railroad house; Lidia's was jam-packed that Friday evening, but we scored a table in the corner of the bar. Owner Lidia Bastianich is a well-known chef with an empire that includes cooking shows and cookbooks in addition to this restaurant, a modern yet cozy take on an Italian farmhouse. As a great consumer of food but not such a great chef, I wasn't familiar with her, but the food made me a fan—once we received it. Pro tip: Never order calzone when you're in a hurry.

The food fest continued the next morning in the form of the Half Fanatics breakfast held in one of the hotel ballrooms. This meant access to hotel lobby bathrooms (no porta-potties!) and staying warm right up until race time—the start line was situated directly in front of the hotel. Impressive as this spread of food may have been, it is a truth universally acknowledged that a power walker must at some point stop consuming calories and start burning them.

Soon we stood in the early morning chill, butt-cheek to butt-cheek in a corral with a bunch of strangers. This being Kansas City, I felt a desperate urge to let out a plaintive moo but wasn't sure the locals would appreciate my pre-dawn humor. Sprung from our corral as the sun rose, we mooooved (sorry) out onto the course. Rumor had it the course had hills, and although the first few miles seemed flat, the buzz among the racers had us concerned.

"There's a big hill near the end that's a killer."

"Save some energy for the hill at Mile 11!"

We traversed tasteful neighborhoods; many of the gorgeous pale limestone homes featured lion and tiger and bear and heaven-knows-what-else statues out front. That's a design feature I've never gravitated toward, but the good folks of Kansas City seem to dig their animal statuary. Other things they love? Art museums, fountains, public art installations … the race route gave us an excellent sampling of all.

At last, we approached the dreaded Mile 11, hoping we'd left

Kansas City, home to the World's Largest Shuttlecock. Photograph by Kellie Bernardez.

enough in the tank to successfully ascend the fearsome hill. Roadside spectators rang cowbells while exhorting, "You got this!" Motivational signs promised us encounters with Ryan Gosling and Brad Pitt on the other side. But as Kellie and I crested the hill, we were laughing, not panting ... and not solely because Ryan and Brad had failed to materialize.

"Wait ... that's it?"

"Seriously, was that the hill?"

My run tracker would later indicate the elevation gain of Mile 11 was 106 feet—the fearsome hill had felt more like a speed bump.

And now I will admit that in my races following Kansas City, I'd smirk scornfully when other folks bemoaned a so-called hilly course. That is until Run the Bluegrass in Kentucky humbled me with its never-ending rollers. It turns out we all have our limits, even those of us who train on hills. Kansas City, I apologize. That's a fine hill you have there; it undoubtedly poses a challenge for many competitors, especially flatlanders who don't have the option of hill training.

But my comeuppance was still months away; in K.C., I crossed the finish line (located next to our hotel) filled with hubris and hungry for chocolate milk. A three-hour drive up I-35 to Iowa awaited—we had the challenge shirts but still needed to complete another half marathon the next day to truly earn them.

Iowa

DES MOINES MARATHON (HALF)

This is a tale about manners, or perhaps a lack thereof. A tale of medals, of power (walking), of spies, and as always, a tale of food.

As our story begins, two women (Kellie and I) enter the lobby of the Des Moines Marriott to find it festooned with the flags of many nations. Around us, conversations in foreign tongues swirl among a crowd that exudes a distinct international flair. A massive banner announces something called the World Food Prize. Could this be a surprise celebration in my honor, recognition of my amazing intake abilities? Indeed not; we learn that this prestigious annual award salutes achievement in global food security rather than individual efforts in consumption.

With food at the forefront of our minds, we quizzed the concierge for local restaurant reviews before offloading our gear. The journey after that morning's Kansas City Marathon had included just one stop—the Iowa Events Center to pick up our swag for the Des Moines Marathon. As with the pullover hoodies we received in K.C., Des Moines provided something a little snazzier than the typical race shirt—a zip jacket that might come in handy as an extra layer given the frigid temperatures forecast for the next morning. Now it was time to refuel at Centro, the nearby Italian place that had been recommended. Devouring the outstanding Italian food didn't stop our eyes from being diverted by the sight of some alluring French fries; we vowed a return the next day.

Sub-freezing cold was as effective a wake-up call as any double

They grow 'em big in the Midwest. Photograph by Kellie Bernardez.

espresso might have been when we hustled to the start line a few blocks from the hotel the next morning. Once underway, we wound through parks, around a lake, past some cute neighborhoods, the flat course leaving us with plenty of available oxygen for conversation, including a discussion of the local attractions along the way.

Around Mile 3, I mentioned to Kellie, "I might try running a Mainly Marathons series sometime ... not eight states in eight days like some people, but it sounds like a good way to try three in a row." Soon we heard a voice behind us.

"Hey, I hope you don't mind me joining in. I overheard you talking about Mainly Marathons. I've done a few of those series and really enjoyed them." Introducing herself as Beth, our new friend went on to extol the virtues of the races. "It's such a well-organized experience, an incredible amount of fun. But the best part is you get to know the other competitors so well. Seeing the same people day after day, you become a family, and I've made lifelong friends."

Beth's enthusiasm was evident; she made a great ambassador for the series. The miles ticked by quickly, her conversation a welcome distraction from my tired legs as we approached the last few miles of our second race in two days.

Then Kellie said, "You know, I'm feeling pretty good, I want to run to the finish."

"Go for it—see you there," I told her, and off she went.

My own pace was increasing, or maybe Beth was slowing down … would it be rude to pull away? Should I say something or keep surging ahead? Knowing she likes to make friends at races and intuiting that she had traveled here by herself, I thought it felt awkward to simply take off. Kellie and I have an understanding that we can each do our own thing during a race. But when you connect with a stranger on the course, what's the etiquette? As I debated slowing my pace or telling her that I was moving on, the rubber band stretched until it finally snapped, and I lost contact with Beth.

Crossing the finish line a couple of miles later I felt wiped out, a little guilty, but happy to receive two medals—one for the Des Moines race plus another for the I-35 Challenge. Kellie and I reconnected; we waited for several minutes hoping to catch Beth as she finished the race but couldn't find her. Beth, if you ever read this, I'm sorry if I kind of blew you off during that race. I hope to see you at a Mainly Marathons event sometime.

You know how sometimes when you discover something new it suddenly seems to pop up everywhere? Kellie, energized by our après-race French fry splurge, elected to tour Des Moines while I tackled some homework for a class I was taking on food writing. One assignment: devouring a fascinating *New Republic* essay titled "Corn Wars," a farcical tale involving the FBI, Chinese spies, hybrid proprietary corn seeds sewn into coat linings, and, believe it or not, the World Food Prize. Imagine … those folks quaffing cocktails downstairs the previous evening might have been secret agents! Des

Moines, Iowa—the epicenter of excellent fries, friendly half marathoners, and international espionage.

Oklahoma

ROUTE 66 MARATHON (HALF), TULSA

Lord, please don't let this guy kill me. Intentionally or not.

I stared out the car window, though nothing punctuated the darkness save an occasional truck taillight. My Uber driver was a Woody Harrelson look-alike; I hoped he had a better driving record than I imagined Woody's to be. Thankfully he didn't try to engage me in conversation on our endless drive through the empty Oklahoma countryside. That left me to conduct my backseat prayer vigil uninterrupted by small talk. I'd decided against taking a couple of puddle-jumpers to Tulsa, opting instead for a direct flight to Oklahoma City. Ubering the two hours to Tulsa had sounded more relaxing than renting a car, but too late I realized that putting my life into the hands of Fake Woody hardly made for the mellow pre-race experience I envisioned. As with foxholes, there are no atheists in a sketchy Uber.

Let me arrive safely in Tulsa, I prayed. *And if I make it ... if it's not too much to ask ... could my race packet please be waiting for me at the hotel?*

Mercifully we arrived at the Aloft Hotel without incident, although it took Fake Woody a few loops around the modernistic property to find the front door. The night shift clerk located my swag bag—once again, a kind stranger came through for me, this time a member of the 50 States Half Marathon Club who picked up my goodies at the expo. In my room at last, I was delighted to find not only my bib but a beautiful race jacket, a neck gaiter, and some mittens, all of which I'd use the next day as the forecast promised sub-freezing morning temperatures. I got into bed right away, hoping I might manage about four hours of dozing.

Sleep before a race is, for me, like sleep before catching a plane:

brief naps interspersed with jolts of clock-checking panic. The next morning my resultant brain grogginess was quickly wiped clean by the 17-degree wind chill factor that assaulted me as I stepped outside. I silently congratulated myself for choosing a hotel a few short blocks from the Half Fanatics meet-up area, where I immediately sought out their heated tent. As a Half Fanatic club exclusive event, Route 66 spoiled us not solely with the tent but also special medals plus post-race food and beer. Scoring a chair close to a heater, I basked in the last warmth I'd feel for hours, grudgingly rising when coaxed to join the club's group photo. It wasn't until the last possible moment that I tore myself away from the tent's warm embrace ... and what was this at my corral entrance, a mirage? No—a Jimmy John's. This bit of serendipity would mollify my typical post-race quest to locate a spot within hotel walking distance for expeditious consumption of much-needed protein.

The first six miles of the route traversed the kind of neighborhoods that made me wish I'd never left the Midwest for the West Coast; I could envision myself living in any of these houses from the cozy cottages to the palatial estates. Thoughts of Meghan Daum's hilarious book *Life Would Be Perfect If I Lived in That House* crossed my mind as I hustled past the homes. That book title summarizes my relationship with real estate and my vast appreciation of race routes that feature residential neighborhoods. They needn't be upscale; my requirements are that they are cute, or brimming with character, or do something to trigger my inner FOMO (Fear of Missing Out). I was struck with an urgency to list my house for sale so that I might achieve the true fulfillment I absolutely *know* can only be attained by purchasing the perfect place.

My imaginary future neighbors had gathered outside as athletes overtook their tree-lined streets. Crowd support along the course was truly overwhelming, especially at legendary Boozers' Bend where it appeared the locals were having even more fun than the competitors. They'd set up a selfie station featuring a winter backdrop as artificial snow blew all about; shotskis were on offer to those in need of something to warm their innards. At that moment the bitter chill killed my phone battery; afraid of meeting the same fate if I didn't keep moving, there were no selfies or shotskis for me.

As much as the first half of the race route was bracingly beautiful, the final miles were a freezing cold sufferfest with icy winds blowing off the Arkansas River. Route 66 was that rare situation where I ended up colder than when I started; my feet had become blocks of ice attached to frozen tree stump legs. Perhaps that was a net positive, providing a welcome dulling of my pain receptors. I thrilled to the site of the Aloft Hotel—the end (of the race, not me) was near! But we kept going ... and going ... and going. It seems my pre-race planning had fixated on lodging near the start line, not the finish. The dawning realization that I'd be retracing all of those steps back to the hotel might have caused tears of anguish but for the knowledge that frozen water on my face would serve to worsen my situation.

Part of my brain had frozen as well, the part that should have had me seeking out the club tent after the finish line. Instead, upon receipt of my medal, I made a beeline for the general race food tent, where my icy claws managed to hoist a slice of pizza to my face while trudging back to the hotel. The walk to the Aloft felt as long as the ride to Tulsa the night before; this time I worried not about crazed Uber drivers but about toppling over thanks to my unbending extremities. But once thawed out in the shower I summoned the motivation to walk the few blocks over to Jimmy John's. Alas, this would mark what I decided would be my final rendezvous with Jimmy; I subsequently discovered he participates in a hobby that doesn't mesh with my values, so I couldn't see giving him my support any longer. So long, Number Four, wheat, easy mayo, with a side of Thinny Chips.... I'll miss you.

The Route 66 race lived up to its reputation as a can't-miss experience, even with the logistical complications and freezing conditions. But I was more than ready for one more Uber ride, the one that would take me to the airport ... this time, the Tulsa airport ... for a direct flight home to warmer climes.

2019

Hawaii	*North Dakota*
Kentucky	*South Dakota*
Tennessee	*North Carolina*
Kansas	*Virginia*
Nebraska	*New Hampshire*
Maryland	*Maine*
Delaware	*Massachusetts*
Pennsylvania	*Vermont*
New Jersey	*South Carolina*
Minnesota	*Georgia*

Hawaii

MAUI OCEANFRONT MARATHON (HALF), LAHAINA

It's equivalent to saying, "I don't like puppies" or "I hate babies," a nearly sacrilegious opinion. But the truth is I'm not a huge Hawaii fan. I'm fully aware of how incredibly privileged I am to have had the opportunity to visit the place, and it's not that I *dislike* Hawaii ... honest. It's just that I'm not a tropical island kind of gal. My dream vacation location is more along the lines of New York City or London than a place known for seafood (I'm allergic), humidity (ugh), and sand (nasty!). Even all of that relaxing quickly becomes too much of a good thing.

When I considered committing to the 50 States Half Marathon challenge, one of the things that made me think *"this ain't never gonna happen"* was the idea of traveling to Hawaii. Flying over water ranks even higher on my thanks-but-no-thanks list than humidity. But with a 25th wedding anniversary approaching, the idea of revisiting Todd's and my honeymoon locale on Maui held some romantic appeal. Our son Derek was graduating from college in May; who knew when we'd take a family vacation together again? And yeah, there was that whole 50 states thing…

That's how I found myself on the start line at the Maui Oceanfront Marathon—but not until I'd spent a few days hanging out at brewpubs and beaches. This was in direct opposition to my preference for an athletic event to take place early in the trip; it's way more fun to race first then let yourself go for the duration of the vacation. But scheduling complications necessitated racing on our last day on Maui, so I tried, and mostly failed, to stick to a healthy pre-race eating and exercise plan. In favor of race day travel, however, I can attest that it's highly motivating to keep a good pace when you know that slacking off means missing your flight home or, at the very least, a long, relaxing shower.

Our four days leading up to the race involved serious caloric consumption (including visits to both locations of Maui Brewing Company) and some quality time at urgent care (thanks to Derek's sea urchin-jellyfish double whammy) plus a few only-in-Hawaii endeavors. Ambitious Todd rented a bike for a ride up and down windy Haleakala, where he was literally blown over at the top; that confirmed the wisdom of my choice to read a book on the beach that day. Our trip coincided with the annual Women's March held at the University of Hawaii Maui College. What I had envisioned as a low-key way of getting a few pre-race miles into my legs ended up being an ambling two-block stroll; on the positive side, at least it didn't sap my energy reserves.

The race director was a terrific communicator, sending waves of emails in the weeks before the big day. Many of those messages claimed that any pre-race problem solving would necessitate bribes of wine, beer, and limes; packet pick-up was happening at the guy's condo in Kihei. His *condo*? Race expos are usually held in some hotel meeting room or convention center, not what sounded like a beachside bachelor pad. The experience turned out to be festive

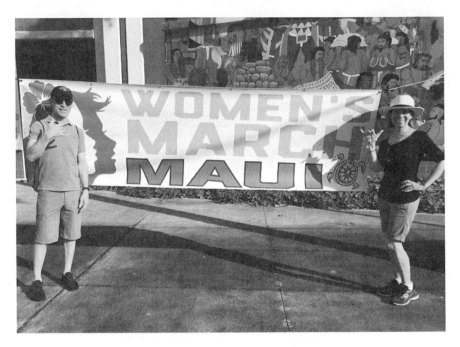

Todd and me prior to a very short training walk.

rather than frightening, staffed by a cadre of non-scary, helpful volunteers. Other competitions offered during race week included a free cookie run; this race director went out of his way to create a fun and friendly experience.

It was wonderful that the race's start area was located at The Shops at Wailea, an easy walk from our base at the Fairmont Kea Lani. Too bad that was for the full marathon; the start line for the half was 45 minutes away. Oops. But finding street parking in Lahaina on race morning was easy; at about 600 participants the field was not too big, not too small, and I felt myself being swept up in the pre-race party atmosphere. Several of the people in attendance were completing their 50th state that day; with each assigned bib number 50 in recognition of their achievement, they were easy to spot either by number or by their obvious (and contagious) excitement.

The course was gorgeous but not the kind that earns a spot at the top of my favorite race scenery list. It was a lot like those Colorado mountains except this time it was waves—captivating to be sure, but also redundant. The route featured many miles that hug the beach, and while that particular spectacle may not be my thing, I appreciated the ocean breezes keeping the dreaded humidity in check. It's an out-and-back course, so if you enjoyed the waves in the first half, you'll like 'em in the second half, too. There were plenty of aid stations staffed by enthusiastic volunteers, so no one was in danger of tropical dehydration.

Once that mermaid-themed medal was around my neck, I scooped up a donut from the snack table plus a few other goodies then sped back to the hotel; I knew my guys would be worried about making it on time to the airport. Thanks to my warp speed efforts we arrived at the gate just as our plane boarded. Finally, I could relax a little ... a very little ... after all, I still had several hours of armrest clutching ahead of me. With the hurdle of Hawaii out of the way I'd checked state #25 off my list—I was officially halfway to my 50-state racing destination.

Kentucky

Run the Bluegrass, Lexington

Marketed as "the Prettiest Race in America," I was mighty curious to see for myself how Run the Bluegrass would stack up against the many scenic courses I've enjoyed. My journey to Kentucky wasn't so pretty—with no direct flights from home, my connection out of Chicago was one of those 40-seater planes that bobble way too much in the best of weather. And this was most assuredly not the best of weather; a serious storm had set its sights on Lexington. So I was greatly relieved to arrive safely, connect with Kellie, then visit the race expo.

"Uh oh!"

Kellie's anguished voice rose above the buzz of the crowd at the historic Keeneland horse racing facility. The problem causing her consternation was easy to identify: a prodigious display of bright, shiny finisher medals. Because she hates to see medals before the finish line, we hurried past—only to realize they were exhibited throughout the expo. When we finally resigned ourselves to the inevitable and took a closer look, I decided this medal was among my favorites. Honoring local horse-made-good, 2018 Triple Crown winner Justify, it met that all-important criterion: a medal design indicative of where the race took place.

The other item as prominently displayed as the medals was bourbon, bourbon, and more bourbon. I wasn't tempted to sample the goods, but the organizers did serve up one possibly irresistible enticement: a sneak preview of the shirts for the following year's 10th-anniversary race. I loved the long-sleeved shirts we received that day with their soft tech fabric in a marvelous shade of medium blue, but the 2020 shirts were going to be Capital-F Fabulous: a blue and white checkerboard design running down the sides that served as an homage to the silks of legendary racehorse Secretariat.

Run the Bluegrass starts at the incredibly civilized hour of 9:00 a.m.—perfect for dealing with that brutal three-hour time difference from the West Coast. But as power walkers who'd need three hours to complete the course, we'd be returning to the hotel past the typical noon check-out time. So thank you, Griffin Gate Marriott, for the 2:00 p.m. late checkout. If only all hotels were as accommodating, so participants wouldn't feel stressed out during their race about quickly returning to the hotel, lest they be forced to spend the rest of their day encrusted in sweat.

All week before the race the one thing that scared me more than the idea of flying on a mini-plane was the possibility of traveling all that distance only to have the race black-flagged. Lightning was forecast for race morning; I'd heard too many stories of racers pulled off course during a race due to unsafe weather conditions. It's one thing when that happens in a local race, quite another when you've traveled 3,000 miles. Fortunately, by race morning, the lightning threat had abated; aside from light rain, our single weather challenge was wind—and lots of it.

As each corral of racers approached the start line (too bad the gates were for photo ops only) it was greeted by the bugle call known to horse racing fans as Call to the Post—a clever way to underscore

Hoisting myself onto this horse race starting gate in Kentucky was harder than the half marathon itself. Photograph by Kellie Bernardez.

the race theme. The course was blissfully bucolic and traffic-free: pasture after pasture of grazing horses, fields of vibrant purple clover, graceful homes that brought to mind southern sorority houses … even the barns were painted with unique quilt-style designs.

But along with lots of horses, there were also lots of hills. I've previously admitted to being a bit of a hill snob due to the terrain back home; inclines and declines are part of my everyday training. Usually, when other racers are bemoaning the supposed hills (Kansas City, I'm lookin' at you), I'm inwardly smug. Well, Keeneland knocked the smug right out of me, and by Mile 10, I was ready for the hills to stop—immediately, if at all possible. From the "You've got to be kidding" and "Oh, come on now … another one?" comments I overheard, I sensed I was not alone.

At last, the hills, and the course, reached a merciful end. My reward? Along with that hefty beauty of a medal, there was the nectar of the race gods, chocolate milk. You can have my share of finish line bourbon and brew; leave the chocolate milk for me.

So was Run the Bluegrass America's prettiest half marathon, based on my experience of over 90 lifetime half marathons? It certainly featured idyllic countryside. I'll always prefer urban races, but this race gets top marks for stunning scenery. I don't know that I'd fly all the way across the country to do it again, but then there was that awesome checkered race T-shirt to consider…

Tennessee

KNOXVILLE MARATHON (HALF)

Car games are a time-honored way to pass the time on road trips. On the endless cross-country family vacations of my youth, the license plate game kept us kids from all-out backseat warfare. So as Kellie and I ventured from Kentucky to Tennessee for our next race of the weekend, we devised our own version of the slug bug game, giving each other a (gentle) punch when we spotted a sign announcing an upcoming Cracker Barrel restaurant. Had we kept it up for the entire three hours, one of us might have required medical care upon arrival in Knoxville.

Like me, Kellie has a family member who's downright obsessed with Cracker Barrel, salivating at the mere mention of the place. Spotting one near our hotel, we took it as a sign that Kellie should have her first encounter with those compellingly dense biscuits, front porch rockers, and retro candy offerings. It can be a challenge to choose what to eat between back-to-back competitions; do you eat for recovery or for race prep? My solution, perhaps not surprisingly, is to eat for both. As it turned out, we could have had our pick from seemingly hundreds of Cracker Barrels that popped up along I-75 like so much kudzu.

Passing the town of Rocky Top triggered the long-buried memory of a bluegrass song that I vaguely recalled being associated with some type of sporting event. Taking a brief break from arm punching, I searched for a classic version of "Rocky Top" on my phone, featuring the legendary Carter Family. Between Cracker Barrel sightings and Mother Maybelle's autoharp, this car trip was giving us a real taste of Tennessee.

We arrived at the Knoxville Convention Center expo as the vendors were packing up to leave. Once our bibs were in hand, we sprinted over to the race T-shirt table.

"The small tee I signed up for really does look kinda small," said Kellie. "Maybe I should get the medium?"

"That's fine," the volunteer replied, "or you can take one of each."

Wait … what?

"Yeah," she shrugged, "you can take both if you want."

This was a first … it's the rare race expo that allows exchanges for a different size shirt, but to be offered two shirts? Unheard of. Perhaps it was due to the expo's imminent closing; they didn't want to get saddled with taking unclaimed shirts back to wherever they came from. We decided not to question our good luck, taking the bonus shirt for Isabel back in California.

The Sheraton Four Points hotel was an ideal 10-minute walk to the start line the next morning, far enough to loosen our muscles up a little but close enough that we wouldn't need to avail ourselves of the gear check or porta-potties. The temperature had dropped to a perfect 45 degrees thanks to a storm that blew through overnight, the brisk air somewhat soothing the aches from the previous day's hills. Standing with the pack at the start line, I felt sudden goosebumps. They weren't from the cool air but from a thousand voices raised together in a rousing rendition of "Rocky Top" complete with a highly energized *"Woo!"* each time we sang the chorus. And then we were off...

The early miles of the course took us around the orangey-red brick buildings of the University of Tennessee. I later learned that the crowd at every UT football and basketball game sings you-know-what; whether or not to add the *"Woo!"* is apparently a source of great controversy (I'm squarely in the pro-woo camp). Passing the Tennessee River, we then entered the Sequoyah Hills neighborhood. How can I sum that place up? Not only did I appreciate the distraction of some top-quality real estate, but the level of neighborly enthusiasm rivaled even that of Tulsa's Boozer's Bend. These folks were partying. They were cheering. They were drinking. They were eating. And they were delighted to share their fun, food, and booze with the racers.

Krispy Kreme donuts held out to racers on sticks? Check.

Couches and fire pits for lounging in the yards? Yep.

Bourbon shots? Lots of 'em. Prefer beer? Here you go!

I even got a "You're mah heeero!" from a woman who looked to be about 90 years old and without a doubt living her best life. All that community spirit distracted me from the fact that I felt about 90 years old; the mild rolling hills of this course on top of the non-stop undulations of Kentucky were a literal pain in the rear, but I was having too much fun to care.

All along the race route, we were serenaded by more bands than I've seen even in a Rock'n'Roll series race (on-course "Rocky Top" count = 3). The course eventually wound through a scenic trail before returning to the downtown finish line. There, the Knoxville Marathon turned out to be one of those situations where it's possible to end up heavier than when you started. The food offerings began with my beloved chocolate milk and went up from there in terms of calories, fat, and sugar. We navigated rows of pizza, heaping mounds of chips and energy bars, sodas, and—in a very Tennessee twist—biscuits.

It was a shame that some selections had run out before our arrival. A chatty volunteer who seemed eager to gossip informed us that the fried chicken and donut supplies had been quickly demolished—not that I needed another donut at this point. The volunteer said that race participants had come through the line with their families and friends, all helping themselves to the offerings.

"They tell us to be nice to everyone," groused the frustrated guy, "so it's hard to know what to do. I tried to tell them that the food is reserved for the participants, but then folks gave me the stink eye and took it anyway. There was this one small boy who took six Krispy Kremes all for himself!"

"Well, maybe he'll get sick," Kellie said hopefully as she devoured her pizza. Yeah, that was kind of mean, but also kind of funny.

I love it when a race gives me a feel for the host city, a sense of the local culture. Since I'm usually in and out of these places in a day, little details make the expense and hassle of traveling to faraway states feel worthwhile. Knoxville earned itself a spot high on my list of favorites thanks to the varied course, engaged spectators, and, of course, that little earworm of a tune that stayed stuck in my head for days.

Kansas

RURAL ROUTE 13.1,
ESBON

The Kansas countryside slumbered beneath a cozy gray blanket of fog as Kellie steered our car toward the Rural Route 13.1 half marathon. Suddenly, rising from the haze like a farm country Brigadoon, the town of Esbon materialized before us. But there was no heather on these hills; instead, there were seemingly endless fields of brown stalks and green shoots. Was it wheat? Corn? Soybeans? I chose to imagine it was sunflowers, envisioning the glorious summer scene that would result. (Kudos to Kansas for their state highway signs with the cute sunflower design, right up there with Utah's adorable beehives.)

So how did gals from California and Montana end up in Esbon, population 99? It made a great back-to-back race weekend with the Lincoln Marathon half scheduled for Sunday, so we met up in

Omaha for the three-hour drive to Mankato, Kansas, to spend the night. The neat, clean Crest-Vue Motel gave me childhood vacation flashbacks, although I can't say I recall staying at a place that featured bird-cleaning facilities—as kids we were all about the swimming pool. Several turkey hunters were staying at the motel; I was greatly relieved not to witness a single turkey that had met its demise and was in need of cleaning.

Next door at the Buffalo Roam for dinner, Kellie was intrigued by the menu's walleye offering.

"What's walleye?" she asked.

"It's whitefish," I said. "My dad used to catch walleye."

"Whitefish?"

"Yeah, you know ... whitefish."

Understandably this explanation was somewhat lacking, so Kellie quizzed the waitress.

"It's whitefish," came the reply.

Finally, the restaurant owner was consulted, a man who seemed savvy about fish species. I'd never questioned what whitefish meant. It was kind of like when my mom said we were having roast for dinner, I never asked, "Roast what?" Our job as kids wasn't to question; it was to clean our plates then wash the dishes—preferably without comment. (Kellie gave the walleye a big thumbs up; try it with the onion topping.)

When we picked up our race bibs at the Esbon Community Center the next morning, I was on a mission to find a fellow Half Fanatic I'd seen listed on the club's race calendar. Dale had come from Saskatchewan, usurping any claim Kellie or I might have of traveling to Esbon from the most exotic location. We chatted with Dale plus many other friendly folks, including a Nebraska hog farmer who provided the inside scoop on the Lincoln course we'd be running the next day. It was one of the friendliest pre-race gatherings I've been a part of, with a remarkable sense of community spirit.

Once our field of 26 half marathoners had lined up, a deafening gun crack sent us off into the rolling hills. I'd thought of Kansas as more of a flatland but Esbon's a decently hilly place. Going up and down ... and up ... and down ... the limestone roads, it dawned on me that this could be my first DFL finish; Kellie and I joked about fighting over who'd have the dubious distinction of being the *lanterne rouge*. Eventually we did overtake a few runners and power walkers, so a DFL finish remained a future ignominy. One motivator to keep up a good pace was the lack of on-course bathroom facilities, with barely a bush to hide behind in case of emergency.

As I took possession of my medal at the finish line, a farmer standing nearby asked, "Ya know what that is, don't cha?"

"Yeah," I replied, "it's a cow ear thingy!" undoubtedly dazzling him with a knowledge of cattle exceeded only by my knowledge of fish. When he exclaimed, "Not everyone would know that!" I had to confess I'd seen it the night before on the race's Facebook page. This medal with baling twine serving as a ribbon truly makes a statement as to the race's venue.

Then it was time to dig into the home-cooked food some local folks had provided, egg casserole, pumpkin cake with cream cheese frosting, and other homemade temptations the big races can't offer. Another important item on our agenda was selecting the perfect piece of limestone from the Paint Your Own Medal table. The following day this souvenir would set off a small panic among TSA agents at the Omaha airport, forcing me to unpack my suitcase as they sought out the scary sharp object I was transporting. I've had my carry-on bag pulled aside for inspection more times than I can count after a race weekend; without fail it's the medals that draw scrutiny.

Is there a medal for the most-unique medal?

125

In the middle of everything (in the Lower 48). Photograph by Kellie Bernardez.

Is it wrong that I feel a sweet sense of revenge knowing that the agents will have to rifle through my sweaty race clothes to unearth them? Here's a tip: If you want to avoid the TSA pawing your panties, carry your medals in a separate bag from your clothes or pack them where they can be easily accessed.

After checking out of the Crest-Vue we were off to Lincoln, but we had an important stop to make along the way—proof that we weren't in the middle of nowhere but smack dab in the center of the continental United States.

I wish there'd been an opportunity to visit the World's Largest Ball of Twine, but it was time for us to follow the sunflower signs to Nebraska.

Nebraska

LINCOLN MARATHON (HALF)

When I had returned to school a couple of years earlier, I'd been motivated in part by a desire to expand my literary horizons. I'd fallen into a rut, favoring books on the same subjects or by the same authors. I'm sorry to say I still haven't read the works of the great Willa Cather, but at least I can now say I've been to her house.

Departing Kansas for our date with the Lincoln Marathon, Kellie and I made a stop right over the Nebraska state line at Red Cloud. A big Cather fan, Kellie didn't want to miss checking out the town where she'd grown up. The scheduled tour time had passed, but the kindly guide at the National Willa Cather Center took us for a private showing of the house. I got the sense this could be a grown-up version of the Laura Ingalls Wilder books I'd loved as a child; Cather's *My Ántonia* now has a spot on my to-read list.

As the tour concluded, our guide suggested we avoid the interstate by taking the more scenic state highway to Lincoln. We'd already seen plenty of farms the past two days; we were about to see a whole lot more. Along with viewing countless fields of what I assume was corn (this was the Cornhusker State, after all), I kept an eye out for the thunderstorms predicted to roll in that evening. All that corn, the looming specter of rain, and whaddaya know, we had ourselves a road trip theme song—Luke Bryan's "Rain Is a Good Thing." I suspect that after being subjected to my repeated renditions of this tune, Kellie was ready for a shot of the whiskey that Mr. Bryan informed us rain and corn combine to create. And I'm sorry to tell you this, Luke, but for half marathoners worried about races being black flagged due to lightning, rain's a *bad* thing.

The Marriott Cornhusker not only hosted the race expo but also had the advantage of being situated a short walk from the start line on the University of Nebraska campus. With our predicted finish times placing us in the race's last wave (wait, this is Nebraska— no corrals?), we lingered at the hotel the next morning until the 7:00 a.m. gun time. Arriving at the start with plenty of time to do some pre-race stretches on the indoor practice field of the Huskers football

127

team, I envisioned absorbing some of their athletic superpowers via the turf. The 7:35 a.m. wave sent us on our way through a campus that was decked out in multitudes of resplendent trees sporting showy springtime flowers.

Next up were some beautiful homes to ogle; all that head swiveling keeps my neck and shoulders from getting stiff during a race. (That's probably not true, but it's how I justify gawping at real estate.) The good citizens of Lincoln embodied the day's Cinco de Mayo spirit by offering to share pitchers of margaritas, even setting out chairs for participants who might opt to party rather than race. Good thing it was Mile 4; at Mile 11, it might have been a more difficult decision.

We navigated through local parks and several scenic neighborhoods until our arrival back on campus for a finish on the 50-yard line of Memorial Stadium. Even this football non-fan was awed by the immense structure. I tried and miserably failed to replicate the Heisman Trophy pose as I ran across the line, but Kellie and I made up for it in the end zone, where we busted out our best touchdown moves. Another finisher, slumped over in apparent pain, called out to us.

"I don't know how you can dance around after finishing a race," she wheezed. "I can barely move."

"Check back with me in an hour or two," cracked Kellie, knowing we'd soon be walking on legs as flexible as corncobs.

With our finisher's bling around our necks, we went in search of sustenance. I scored my much-loved chocolate milk; Kellie was thrilled to discover a cache of Fritos.

"This was my pregnancy food craving!" she gushed enthusiastically.

I had to ask. "You cannot possibly mean Fritos washed down with chocolate milk?"

"Oh yeah."

This sounded as appalling a combo as the legendary pickles and ice cream, but given that her son is now a handsome, successful adult, it's evidently a pre-natal recipe for success.

We parted ways that afternoon; Kellie was off to Montana, but I wasn't going home just yet. I had a date in Tempe to pick up another kind of swag—a master's degree diploma from Arizona State University. When I decided to return to school at age 59, I heard a question repeatedly from friends and family: "What are you going to do with it?" Obtaining this degree wasn't so I could do something *with* it; it was about the journey and the destination, not some magical aftermath. Much like the 50-states goal, the value was in the enjoyment of what I learned along the way, the impact it had on me, and the sheer exhilaration that comes from setting and then achieving a difficult goal. As with the hardest race courses, the most fearsome academic courses often turned out to be the most satisfying to conquer. The next day in Arizona I'd cross the scholastic finish line; in this case, the stage at Wells Fargo Arena, my academic journey now complete.

Delaware

Mainly Marathons Independence Series, Bear

"I'm not here to make friends."—Every reality show villain ever

Flitting around the country for half marathons is admittedly not the most eco-friendly fitness pursuit; my guilt over contributing to climate change via so much air travel made the Mainly Marathons series a very intriguing option. This traveling race caravan offers events in adjacent states on consecutive days, creating more stress on my body in exchange for less stress on the climate. By now I'd heard so many stories about the incredible camaraderie at these races, the lasting friendships that are forged ... it all sounded perfect for any solo race traveler who covets connection or for enthusiastic extroverts.

Now I have a confession: As much as I like making new pals, that's not my primary consideration at a race. As a relatively shy, introverted type, for me it's a real stretch to chat up groups of strangers. The benefit of Mainly Marathons' highly touted *esprit de corps* wasn't a major enticement for me, but the idea of knocking off several states with a single round trip was too tempting to pass up.

My East Coast sojourn began with a literal bang—hitting a car when I pulled into a parking spot at the San Francisco airport. Seeing nothing of concern, I still spent the entire trip wondering if I'd return to an accident claim (I didn't). On this day I'd be flying United Airlines rather than my preferred Southwest; "carry-on" is not a concept United fully accommodates. Maybe the first 50 or so passengers are allowed a carry-on bag while Group 4 and 5 types such as myself are forced to gate check. When traveling to a race lost bags aren't an inconvenience but a potential disaster; United's propensity for gate checking prompted me to start wearing running shoes on planes just in case. That's not typically my style, although I still found myself among the best-dressed passengers as that particular bar is set quite low.

Not willing to pay half my retirement savings for WiFi, I settled in to watch a free movie. Suddenly a flash flood rushed toward me, its stream drenching my purse as it made its way toward my feet. The passenger in front of me had placed a full soda can beneath her seat; the can immediately toppled, spreading its contents. While running to the galley for towels I alerted a flight attendant who helped me to sop up the mess. Upon receiving a lecture from the flight attendant, the culprit poked her head around the seat, uttering a halfhearted "sorry." Well, at least that was more than I got from the oblivious guy who poured burning hot coffee all over my new sweater on the previous year's flight to Chicago.

The Nissan Versa I picked up at Hertz in Philadelphia showed a mere 13 miles on the odometer, prompting an unhappy flashback to 1982 and my brand-new jade green Chevy Cavalier. Among its many fine features were a non-functional heater (this was Michigan in February) and a broken brake shoe that stranded me in an intersection during a midnight snowstorm on my first evening of ownership. In other words, new car doesn't always equal no problems. Fingers crossed, I drove to Delaware.

My greeting at the Sheraton fell well short of those super-friendly Bonvoy ads.

2. 50 States and Washington, D.C.

"What's your last name?" snapped the desk clerk.

I told her.

"Sign here."

I signed.

"Here's your key."

Well, the check-in process was efficient, I'll give her that. Ten words total and I was in my room.

Race #1 in Mainly Marathons' Independence Series was in Bear, Delaware—the name serving as a clue to the rural nature of the course. As promised, the group of about 200 runners and walkers was a very welcoming bunch. Several of them seemed to be friends of long-standing, judging by the joyous reunions occurring all around me. We proceeded to traverse six loops of a muddy course; the forecast thunderstorms held off but might have felt better than the oppressive humidity that was styling my hair into an ever-frizzier halo with each step. By race's end, my car's vanity mirror reflected the frightening visage of a woman who bore a great resemblance to Bernie Sanders if Bernie were to don Lycra capri tights then roll to and fro in mid–Atlantic mud.

I try not to dwell on the aging process, but honestly, I can't handle Aquafina. Not the comedienne (Awkwafina is hilarious) but the bottled water. That's the brand this hotel (and the entire Marriott chain) carried; I hadn't yet had time to buy a case of water at a local store. So when my Dirty-Bernie self entered the Sheraton lobby, I had to ask the desk clerk for help with opening the bottle I'd purchased; as happened on my flight home from my Ohio race, I could not get the thing to budge. She shot me a look that said, *"I can tell there's a Trip Advisor review hinging on this."* Pausing, she heaved a sigh, stated, "I'm extremely germaphobic...," then proceeded to construct a hazmat suit out of Kleenex before cracking it open. It's a good thing for her we were still many months away from the onset of a global pandemic.

Now ashamed of both my weakness and my apparent cooties, I skulked up to my room for a much-needed shower. But when I finished, the faucet wouldn't budge; steaming water continued to blast forth. Was this yet again the fault of my old lady hands? As the room

Lush, leafy, and oh-so-humid Delaware.

transformed into a sauna, I ran for the telephone to call the front desk only to discover that it, too, was inoperable. Finally reaching her from my cell phone, Ms. Germophobe sent up a maintenance man who determined that the faucet was every bit as busted as the phone. I wasn't thrilled about having a random guy working in my room but at least it meant I hadn't lost my ability to turn off a faucet.

Attempts to flat iron the humidity out of my hair were fruitless; still resembling Senator Sanders (albeit on one of his better days), I went for a drive around the University of Delaware campus. I spotted the public policy center named for famous alum Joe Biden; since I seemed to be morphing into Bernie, I was surprised not to start waggling a pointed finger while delivering a lecture on progressive politics. Instead, I returned to the hotel to rest, hoping to preserve some energy for the upcoming three half marathons in the next three days.

Maryland

Mainly Marathons Independence Series, Elkton

I'm always appreciative when people have said kind things about my effort to run a half marathon in every state. But then I think—if they only knew about the people I've met along the way who are performing feats far more impressive than mine.

The course for Race #2 of the Independence Series wasn't far over the Maryland border, allowing for a second night at my Delaware hotel. Sequential nights in the same place are a luxury on these back-to-back race trips, one less day of packing and unpacking. The scene was similar to the previous day's contest; the storm that had passed through overnight had done nothing to alleviate the suffocating mugginess. A muddy trail took us through a forested area into an opening with wider vistas, nice enough for the first few laps, but by loop three of seven, I felt desperate for distraction. After crossing paths with the other participants so often, I learned which ones to avoid—for example, the guy I dubbed Sir Farts-a-Lot or shirtless (and not shy about it) Harry Backman. But then I discovered that there were some competitors with shirts (and thank you for wearing one!) that weren't merely your typical race togs but actually told a story.

Yes, race shirts provided a distraction from my thoughts of

Power Walk!

"What does poison ivy look like again?" and *"Oh yeah, aren't the wooded areas on the East Coast infested with Lyme Disease–bearing ticks?"* When I noticed the jersey worn by one competitor, I realized I was in the presence of either greatness or madness—possibly both. His shirt announced his status as a Global Marathon Challenger; every day of this race series, he was setting a new world record for most full marathons run in one year and this particular day was #281. I didn't envy the amount of effort he was putting forth to accomplish this feat, but I was insanely jealous of the amount of food he surely got to eat every day. His ultimate goal: 1,000 full marathons in four years.

Then there was another runner chalking up a daily marathon during this series. A Navy veteran of the Iraq War, he had sustained life-threatening injuries when a roadside bomb detonated. The Purple Heart recipient nearly lost a leg and was told he'd never run again yet here he was, crushing the course while carrying a large American flag every step of the way. The story of his remarkable recovery was briefly outlined on the back of his shirt, but he'd literally put the past behind him. His takeaway from that life-changing experience was to drop the idea of bucket lists, choosing instead to focus on achieving goals now, not in the future. He knew all too well that tomorrow isn't guaranteed to anyone.

Those repeated loops gave me an unexpected gift. Rather than allowing myself to be distracted by scenery, I had the opportunity to look inward, finding myself in an almost meditative state. The grit of those two men, their optimism and determination, shifted something inside of me that dreary day. True, it wasn't my favorite kind of weather or course, but how incredibly privileged was I to have the opportunity to be out here? I had the financial wherewithal and family support to take trips like this. I had two functional legs, a heart, and two lungs that gave me what I asked of them and more. I took their *carpe diem* attitude to heart, vowing to complete as many races as I could for the remainder of 2019. Little did I know then that there was a worldwide crisis in the offing that would even further increase my determination to take advantage of the here and now.

Pennsylvania

MAINLY MARATHONS INDEPENDENCE SERIES, BIRDSBORO

And now, a public service announcement for iPhone owners: Did you know that when your phone is in Do Not Disturb mode, you'll still receive government alerts unless you specifically opt-out? I learned that lesson the hard way when I was jolted from a sound sleep by a blasting flash flood warning. Waiting for my pulse to return to normal as thunder rattled my hotel room window, I contemplated the storm's potentially dire effects on the race that was starting in a mere five hours.

Two half marathons in as many days had left me feeling wrung out; I was too tired to be much of a tourist on the previous day's drive from Delaware to Pennsylvania. But I love colleges, and you can't throw an SAT prep book in Western PA without hitting a campus or three. After a quick drive around Villanova University, I strolled (okay, limped) through a campus that tops many a "most beautiful" list—Bryn Mawr College. I took in the serene summertime vibe, and the empty pathways conjured ghosts of coeds past; I imagined them strolling by, books clutched to Bobbie Brooks–clad bosoms that remained chastely unpawed by the Haverford College boys up the road. I wish I'd had the energy to tour Haverford, Swarthmore, Lehigh, and other schools but energy conservation for the next two days of racing was my top priority.

By the time I departed my hotel the next morning the overnight storm had lessened to gentle rain. Siri guided me toward our race location, the Daniel Boone Homestead in Birdsboro. I wasn't terribly concerned when she took me past a few park entries; most appeared gated, so I assumed she was leading me to an open entrance. My anxiety increased when I was led away from the park, down a single lane road ... and suddenly up ahead, nearly concealed by the predawn darkness, a river appeared where the road was supposed to be. That middle of the night flood warning flashed through my mind as water coursed across the pavement at a furious rate. There wasn't room for a simple U-turn on the narrow road; by the time I executed

135

a nine-point turn, two new rivers had materialized seemingly from nowhere over the section of road I'd just passed.

There wasn't time to contemplate my limited options. Gunning the engine, I held my breath and barreled through the flood; I didn't exhale until confirming that my brakes were still functional when I reached the other side. But I was still faced with a dilemma—how to get into the park. Retracing my route, this time I found an open entrance. The problem now was the many runners and walkers who had taken over the road.

"Is this the way to the start?" I called out to one guy.

He eyed me with suspicion. "Are you in the race?"

A logical question, I suppose, although I wanted to ask, "What else would I be doing out here at 5:50 a.m.?" Although there were a mere 10 minutes before the regular start time, I had to cautiously thread my way through the many people already dotting the road who had opted for the 5:00 a.m. early start.

Finally locating a parking spot, I asked someone which way I should go—people were heading in both directions. The answer came back: "Turn right." Well, yes, that would have been the way to go if I were in the race, but it added a half-mile to my trek to the start line. As it was now past 6:00, I started truckin' at a good clip.

"Nice pace!" someone shouted.

"Looking good!" came further encouragement.

"I haven't even started the race yet!" I yelped back.

Finally arriving at the scorer's table, I started my Garmin watch at 06:09:30 on the official race clock. My lingering adrenaline from the morning's near-disaster fueled a terrific pace for my first few miles. I navigated my way around puddles and mud galore thanks to the overnight weather theatrics, but luckily some sections of the course were paved. Once I turned my attention to the surroundings of the Homestead, I realized that I knew little about Daniel Boone aside from the fact that Fess Parker had starred in a television show about the guy when I was a kid; the theme song played on heavy rotation in my brain throughout the race.

Checking in with the scorer's table once again at the finish, I was asked if I started at 6 a.m. or with the 5 a.m. early start.

"My start time was 6:09:30," I replied.

That sparked no sympathy from the scorer, who marked me as starting at 6 a.m. So it became, on the official records, my all-time slowest half marathon to date. That was okay by me; I'll take a slow race time over a fast trip down a river in a rental car any day.

New Jersey

Mainly Marathons Independence Series, Branchville

BridgeGate, bankrupt casinos, mobsters ... that's some of what comes to mind when I think of New Jersey. Prior sojourns to the state for my college roommate's wedding and the 1992 Miss America Pageant had left an impression of upscale suburbia mixed with unbridled tackiness. I wasn't sure what to expect this time, knowing I'd be running a race in some place called Branchville. But to find out, I had to get there.

I avoid taking medicine, but after three half marathons in three days my body had the flexibility of a poker chip; a dose of vitamin I (Ibuprofen) was definitely called for. It worked well enough to get me into the car and on the road but without the oomph necessary to explore Pennsylvania Dutch country. The road signs for horse-drawn buggies raised my hopes of spotting some Amish folks but, sadly, no sightings materialized. I am just immature enough to have been amused by the signs pointing to Virginville, wondering if it bore any relationship to the town I'd passed through two days earlier: Blue Ball, Delaware.

The high point of the day's journey arrived when I stopped for gas on the other side of the state line, rejoicing in the knowledge that New Jersey doesn't allow self-service. Thank you, Lord, for sparing me the need to haul my aching body from the car. Such a joy it was to merely pull up to the pump, hand my credit card over to the pimply-faced teen attendant and say, "Fill 'er up!"

The next morning brought a welcome change in the weather— no, not clear skies, but steady light rain that felt like liquid nirvana compared to the previous stretch of stifling days. The course through lush Stokes State Forest was all paved; puddles lurked everywhere, but at least we weren't glomping through mud. On a route shaped like a bow tie, participants crossed paths with each other 14 times throughout the half marathon. Currently enduring Day Four of this adventure, I must admit I'd lost my enthusiasm for enthusiasm. I'd given more thumbs-up than Donald Trump at a campaign rally. I'd called out more encouraging affirmations than a soccer mom of triplets. Stop being such an old grouch, I told myself; you're lucky to be doing this even if it isn't your idea of a peak experience.

Suddenly around Mile 9, a euphoric feeling washed over me that was every bit as invigorating as that morning rain. I was going to do it ... I was going to finish this race. I suddenly knew in every painful bone and muscle of my body that I was capable of completing these four half marathons in four days. Although I'd known logically that I probably would, until that moment I hadn't truly believed it. And it felt good. It felt as good as that Advil I'd taken at the start of the race. My mood perked up, my pace picked up—I was ready to get this deal over and done.

I didn't stick around for any fond farewells at the finish. Most of the other folks were heading to New York for the fifth and final day of the series; that would have been a repeat state for me, so I was taking a pass. Instead, I needed to get back to the hotel with enough time to wash up and then dry not just myself but my clothes and shoes— no one wants to arrive home with a suitcase stuffed full of moldy, rain-and-sweat-marinated running gear.

At Newark airport for my flight to California, it was my extreme pleasure to experience the Revenge of Boarding Group Four. Our inbound plane had arrived late, meaning the cabin cleaners were still at work. Because they'd started at the rear of the plane, we schlubs seated in the back were boarded before the folks up front. What a thrill to stroll down the jetway, carry-on in hand (no forced gate check, thank you very much), past the glares of the Premiere Platinum Fancy-Pants People. It's the little things, y'all, and if I can't snag a race win I'll settle for victory at the United terminal.

Minnesota

Mainly Marathons Prairie Series, Breckenridge

You know you're not on the most updated of aircraft when the flight attendant tells you, "If that bathroom door opens during the flight, reach over and give it a shove!" On this scary mini-plane from Denver to Fargo, my back row seat placed me directly across a foot-wide aisle from the plane's sole toilet. There were even little ashtrays in the wall where passengers from days of yore would extinguish their cigarettes. What era did this rig date from, anyway? I tried not to think about it, diverting my mental energy to praying that no passenger would be struck with a mid-flight bout of diarrhea.

We arrived in Fargo minus any biohazard episodes, although I did indeed have to smack that door shut a few times mid-flight. One good thing about scary mini-planes is that they take you to mini-airports where rental car pick up is so easy compared to the typical shuttle bus schlep to an off-site rental hub. Within minutes of landing, I was on my way to Wahpeton, North Dakota, home base for two nights. The next day's race would be the first in the Mainly Marathons' Prairie Series lineup. A single route, hugging both sides of the state line, could check either the Minnesota or North Dakota box on a 50-stater's scorecard; we'd use the same course two days in a row.

The driving style here was radically different than at home in the Bay Area. Cars were going 60 in a 55 zone ... and still doing 60 when the speed limit increased to 80. While parts of Minnesota are resplendent with trees and lakes, the terrain here along the western border consisted of vast emptiness somewhat relieved by the occasional silo or field of unknown produce. Either the corn was as high as an elephant's eye, or the soy was as tall as an elephant's ... well, there were crops, okay? With a final turn back into North Dakota, I reached relative civilization. Wahpeton, North Dakota, with its population of 7,000, and sister city Breckenridge, Minnesota, with another 3,000 folks, appeared like quite the metropolis amidst all those fields.

A couple checking in at the hotel ahead of me sported shirts from other marathons. Assuming they must be here for the race, and assuming I'd see them many times over the next few days, I decided to get into the Mainly Marathons spirit and say hello. "Are you here for the race?" I said with a smile. The man glanced at me, glanced back, mumbled a quick "yes" under his breath before turning away; the pair clutched their suitcases then sped off for the elevator. Quite obviously I still had work to do in developing that magic alchemy that binds so many race participants in close friendships.

A small general store stocked with Dasani meant I wouldn't be begging anyone on this trip to open those impossible Aquafina bottles. The local Mexican place sported a festive atmosphere for enjoying my dinner: an entrée of sodium with a side of rice and beans. Back at the hotel, heaving my bloated body onto the bed, I switched on HBO in time for the food poisoning scene from *Bridesmaids*. Transfixed by this highly entertaining bad omen, I burrowed into bedding that reeked of an old man's whiskey-soaked breath, hopeful that sleep would overtake me well before my 4:15 a.m. alarm sounded.

The olfactory assault continued the next day via an intense manure odor that permeated the morning air. A short drive over the state line brought me to the U-shaped circuit of seven laps that would be required for the half marathon. The surroundings were much like any typical municipal park with its swimming pool and baseball field but this one was enlivened by the river that runs through it, the Red River of the North. A big fan of regional accents, I'd noticed that the Mainly Marathons race director, a Minnesota native, had sported a slight accent when we were on the East Coast. Now it was magnified to the 10th power, and I couldn't help but smile when he informed the racers he'd walk us across the state line into "Nooorth Dakoootah" for the start.

A great source of curiosity on this course was a series of bizarre screeching noises that at first sounded like someone encountering either serious pain or scary wildlife. What a relief to learn that the howls were emanating from a nearby zoo—the animals were excited about feeding time, something I could absolutely relate to. The only scary wildlife I encountered that day were the mosquitoes, considered to be the unofficial Minnesota state bird. They welcomed me the way they know best; I gave so much blood I felt like an Olympic athlete undergoing doping control.

Finishing the race felt like less of a relief than normal because I knew I'd be back at the same time, same place the very next day for another seven laps of the same course. I was more than ready for a change of scenery (and smells) but consoled myself with the tradeoff of staying in the same hotel two nights in a row. However, it turned out I was going to have to embark on a little unexpected side trip...

North Dakota

Mainly Marathons Prairie Series, Wahpeton

I try to be smart about race trip prep; that means keeping a list of necessities in my phone so I'm not constantly reinventing the packing list wheel. But somehow the notation about KT Tape had disappeared from that list and darned if I didn't forget to bring some with me. That stretchy athletic tape has been a godsend over the years for my chronic foot arch problem (not to mention securing my left shoe heel lift to my orthotic on rainy days, fixing the occasional broken luggage handle ... it's basically duct tape for athletes). I'd survived the first half marathon in the Prairie Series earlier that day uninjured, but no way was I going to risk another two races without it.

It turns out that Wahpeton not only rolls up their sidewalks on Saturday nights, but they also keep 'em stashed away until Monday morning. That meant the town's sporting goods store was closed, and *that* meant I'd be taking a two-hour round trip back to Fargo, where I'd flown in the day before. I didn't mind too much; our race that morning had started at the unusually early hour of 5:30 a.m. to avoid the midday heat, so by mid-morning I was dressed and ready to roll with the whole day a blank slate waiting to be filled with something fun.

The visit to Fargo gave me an excuse to eat at Jimmy John's. Yeah, yeah.... I'd sworn off eating there when I discovered he's a big game hunter. But I'm weak-willed, and the sandwiches are a comforting known quantity when I'm traveling. I console (or delude) myself with the knowledge that each location is owned by a franchisee; I pretend they're all vegans who donate to PETA. With sandwich eaten and KT Tape procured at the local Target store, I set off to find Fargo's top-rated tourist attraction.

"Make sure I look goofy," I told the person tasked with photographing me alongside the wood chipper from the film *Fargo*. I couldn't exactly recall the scene where Steve Buscemi's body was run through the chipper; no doubt I'd covered my eyes for most of it. But the guy doing the deed must have looked a little deranged, right? For added authenticity, the clerk at the Fargo visitor's center supplied me with an earflap cap, which hopefully hadn't recently seen the head of a lice-bearing tourist. I'm not sure the hat compensated for my Ann Taylor skirt with the sailboat design and Kate Middleton–inspired Superga sneakers in creating a credible look. But since goofy is what I was aiming for, I feel that in its own special way my ensemble aided me in achieving that goal.

The visitor's center gal wore a sweatshirt from North Dakota State University; she told me the place was pretty nice. Never one to turn down an opportunity to visit a college campus, I checked it out. It might not have been Bryn Mawr–level lovely, but it had a certain Midwestern public university charm. It was unquestionably the first campus I'd ever visited that featured its very own livestock arena.

The next morning the air of Wahpeton had a new olfactory assault in store for my nasal passages; yesterday's base layer of manure was joined by top notes of sewage so strong I could taste it. Yesterday's half marathon had checked off the box for Minnesota, the finish line state; today would count for North Dakota, the location of our start line. Seven more laps, three more hours of what baseball legend Yogi Berra allegedly termed "déjà vu all over again." The thing that made this day's slog bearable was reminding myself that tomorrow we'd be on a different course.

In the past I had tended to plan my race trips as surgical strikes— in and out of town quickly, making exceptions for destinations such as New York City and New Orleans. But as my 50-state journey

It doesn't get more Fargo than this.

was evolving, so was I; now I was consciously making an effort to embrace serendipity with stops at any attractions that caught my attention. After picking up my second medal in two days, I knew I couldn't leave Wahpeton without tracking down literally the biggest feature for which it's known, the Wahpeton Wahpper. At 40 feet and

143

The Wahpeton Wahpper in its 40-foot glory.

5,000 pounds, it's said to be the world's largest catfish; one certainly hopes so.

South Dakota

MAINLY MARATHONS PRAIRIE SERIES, BALTIC

The perfect word escapes me.... Lodestar? Touchstone? Neither seems quite right to describe the role Ma Ingalls has played in my life. Not the TV show Ma Ingalls—I never watched *Little House on the Prairie* to avoid memories of my favorite childhood books being tainted by Hollywood's interpretation. No, my Ma Ingalls comes straight from the pen of Laura Ingalls Wilder.

I think of Ma whenever I contemplate a mind-boggling fact of modern life: the moon landing, an iPhone, the Kardashian family.

I imagine Ma exclaiming, "Well, I never..." as her voice trails off in wonderment. I'm not sure why it's Ma I think of. Why not Pa or Laura? For whatever reason, it's Ma who has been a constant, ever-incredulous presence in my life.

Glancing at the map for my drive from North Dakota to Sioux Falls, South Dakota, for Race #3 of the Prairie Series, my eye was caught by the name De Smet; that's the town where the Ingalls family moved in the 1870s. It meant going two hours out of my way, but much like Pa there was no way I was going to pass up making that trek across Dakota Territory.

I felt a bit misty-eyed as I walked through the schoolhouse that Laura attended; it was easy, and so emotionally impactful, to imagine the Ingalls family enduring the hardships of prairie life as I toured the home where her family spent their first winter in De Smet. Admittedly the large herd of children running around crying and shrieking was a bit distracting. I get it—it's not a shrine, it's a place where

Visiting my constant companion, Ma Ingalls, in South Dakota.

145

worn-out kids being hauled around on summer vacations can let off a little steam. I was that kid once, too. But Ma Ingalls would have put paid to that behavior, let me tell you!

I was able to have a private moment with Ma at a cemetery on the outskirts of De Smet. There, sheltered from the prairie winds by a stand of trees, lay the Ingalls family gravestones. I told Ma how much she's meant to me over the years, how, in my own weird way, I'm keeping her memory alive. After spending several quiet minutes viewing their graves and those of some Ingalls family De Smet neighbors, it was time to finish my visit and prepare for another half marathon … a concept I'm sure Caroline Ingalls could not even begin to understand.

The next day's race took place in Baltic, 15 minutes north of Sioux Falls. A mere two weeks earlier the area had been completely underwater due to heavy rain. The sunrise revealed a riverside course that had partially dried out, although some fallen trees were cleared away by a hard-working crew hours before the race's start. As a result, the half marathon course was shrunk down to 13 repetitions of a one-mile circuit. Ugh. Although it made for a less interesting course, ironically that worked to my benefit; the day before I had developed a painful lump on top of my foot that hadn't disappeared overnight as I had hoped. Under normal circumstances, I'd have taken time off to give it a rest—but was I going to call it quits and go home? No, I was not. If a worst-case scenario unfolded, at least with this short loop course I'd never be too far from medical help or a place to sit down.

Distraction was delivered in the form of a fellow power walker who kept pace with me for several miles. Damon was completing 26.2 miles that day in his quest to complete a full marathon in all 50 states—for the third time. His job as a flight attendant helped to pay for all of that travel as did sleeping in his rental car, sometimes in strip mall parking lots. I have so much admiration for the dedicated racers who endure those conditions to achieve their goals. I admit to being spoiled; I'd likely only consider car camping if Honda came out with a model called the Ritz-Carlton that featured a pillow-top bed and restaurant on wheels. Damon's mesmerizing travel tales were more effective than a dose of Tylenol in helping me cope with the foot pain that increased with every mile.

"How do you deal with injuries when you're doing such high mileage?" I asked Damon. "I assume you must develop overuse injuries."

"Well, sure," he replied, "but I push through them. What else can you do?"

What else indeed. No way was I going to stop before I'd finished this race even if I had to limp to the finish. But I got 'er done, with a minor amount of limping required; I picked up my medal, snapped a few photos, then hustled off to catch a noon flight to Denver. (It turns out I had developed a cyst on a metatarsal bone from an overly-tight shoelace. Lesson learned: Always loosen shoelaces all the way to the toe box, then re-lace with a bit of slack.)

On the way out of town, I stopped at a gift shop to pick up a few souvenirs for the folks back home. Debating between a jar of South Dakota Kick-Ass Compote or choke cherry jelly, I decided to consult the lady at the counter; she looked quite neighborly and I could picture her clad in an apron, whipping up provisions to store in the cellar for winter.

"Excuse me, could you tell me what is the difference between jelly and compote?"

"*What?*" she snapped.

"The difference between jelly and compote. These two jars."

"*Lemme see those.*"

She proceeded to squint at the jars for a moment, then rudely shoved them back at me.

"I dunno. Didn't even know we had two different things in those jars. Thought they were all jelly."

With that, she turned away to ring up someone's purchase. As I searched for the answer* on my phone, I could swear I heard Ma Ingalls whisper in my ear, "Don't feel bad, dear. Her great-grandmother was Nellie Oleson."

---

*Compote, made from unstrained boiled fruit with added spices, is slightly liquid in texture and both sweet and savory in flavor; jelly is smooth, clear, and sweet—essentially, spreadable fruit juice.

North Carolina
RACE 13.1,
CHARLOTTE

"I mean it's fine, but it's not a race you'd travel for."

Well. That certainly was an inauspicious intro to the Race 13.1 Charlotte half marathon I'd flown 2,700 miles to attend. This pronouncement of mediocrity was delivered to Kellie and me as we debated the best route from our hotel to the start line. When a guy with a race bib appeared, we tagged along as he walked outside, informing us he'd run this race before—and it wasn't necessarily a favorite.

"I'm from California," I told him, "Kellie's from Montana, so, uh … it's too late now, you know? We already came a long way to be here. What don't you like about the race?"

"It's not that there's anything wrong with it," he replied, "it's just … nothing special."

Now on state #37 of my 50-state quest, I didn't need special; I needed North Carolina done and dusted. While I love humongous events, sometimes it's nice to mix things up a little and experience the smaller, more mellow affairs.

Upon arrival in Charlotte the previous afternoon, we'd gone directly to packet pickup at a sporting goods store. Easy-peasy, no long lines to deal with, then an Italian dinner followed by an early collapse into bed. It was heavenly to have the start/finish area a short walk away the next morning. There were no waves or corrals needed for this field of fewer than 1,000 runners and walkers, but the race offered some amenities typically found at larger events such as pacers to aid in targeting specific time goals. We lined up near the 2:45 pacer, but shortly after the gun went off, I was viewing the back end of the 3:00 pace pack.

"Uh oh. Do you see that?" I asked Kellie.

"I'd like to go sub-three," came her reply, and there we had it: our strategy for the race. In my glory days (all of two years earlier) my half marathon finish times were in the 2:47–2:52 range. But given the number of races I was doing now, I'd dialed back on speed to avoid the extra stress a faster pace placed on my hip flexors and joints. Sub-three sounded perfect to me.

By Mile 3 we were a few steps in front of the pacer, but then we noticed something—our Garmin GPS watches showed we were a few tenths of a mile short of the distance indicated by the on-course mile markers. We didn't know whether to trust our watches, the signs, or the pacer. If she timed her pace according to misplaced signs, she'd finish in over three hours—a pacing sin of the highest magnitude and a bummer for us if we exceeded our time goal.

I was happy that there were no hurricanes bearing down on the Carolinas that week, but the humid air was still heavier than I was used to. With sunny skies and a temperature already rocketing north of 60 degrees, we were grateful that most of the course consisted of tree-shaded trails. A diversion through some leafy neighborhoods brought a welcome change of environment before we turned toward the finish.

Still trying to keep Ms. Three Hour Pacer from breathing down our sweaty necks just past the Mile 12 marker, we entered the Cheering Mile, a human tunnel of cowbell-clanging folks whooping us on to the finish. "Either this is more like a Cheering Half-Mile or those signs are flat-out wrong," I panted. Sure enough, the final "mile" was about 1.25 miles long as road distance reality caught up to the signage. Finishing at 2:58 and change, we asked a nearby finisher to snap our photo with the clock in the background before it rolled over to 3:00:00.

"Yeah," said our photographer friend, "I noticed that, too—the mile markers were so far off! It was killin' me!" She joined us in awaiting the arrival of the pacer, who crossed the line in solitary glory around 3:00:45. Hopefully, she crossed the start line far enough back that her actual chip time was a sub-three.

Our glittery medals featured Charlotte's skyline, as did the race shirts, a bit of false advertising as we were nowhere near downtown at any point during the race. While a downtown route might have raised my race assessment from "fine" to "wow!" this location had the advantage of that short walk back to the Springhill Suites.

The clock strikes 2:59:53 in Charlotte, North Carolina.

Despite the lack of crushing humidity, my hair had gone full Bozo; no way was I going to drive to our next race in Virginia looking like everyone's favorite clown (does anyone actually have a favorite clown?). And don't for a second think there isn't additional pressure to sport presentable hair when your traveling companion also happens to be a professional hairstylist. Late checkout was manna from heaven, but ... when did hotels cease making bathroom fans standard equipment? They are essential for eradicating the moisture after a shower plus providing the all-important sound buffer that allows you to at least pretend your traveling companion isn't listening to all your business on the other side of that paper-thin wall. Hotel bathrooms with fans provide relief in more ways than one—please, hotel chains, bring 'em back.

Virginia

HOKIE HALF MARATHON, BLACKSBURG

"What's a Hokie? I AM." So proclaimed one runner's shirt at the Hokie Half Marathon in Blacksburg—home to Virginia Tech University and some very loyal fans. Half the competitors were clad in the maroon and orange school colors; it may sound garish, but somehow it works. This was far from the sole exhibition of school pride that Kellie and I found around town. We stumbled across statues of the HokieBird mascot around every turn ... Firefighter Hokie, Hokie Pokie Dot, Van Gogh Hokie, even a Lego Hokie standing guard over the shopping center where we received our race swag.

And this race had shirts, plural! We collected white long-sleeved shirts (among my all-time favorites) at the expo, then black short-sleeved finisher shirts at the race finale, both featuring HokieBird tracks in their design. Receiving two shirts greatly increases the odds that at least one will both fit and flatter.

After the expo there was yet another hour to drive; it was Virginia Tech parent weekend, so every hotel room near town had been booked eons ago. Thus we were lodging at the Fairfield Inn 55 miles away in the town of Wytheville (that's pronounced With-ville, y'all). Still famished from our Charlotte half marathon earlier that day, we took the desk clerk's recommendation to dine at the Log House 1776 Restaurant. As the name implies, it was founded the same year as our

Kellie cozies up to Lego Hokie at the expo in Virginia.

nation; the log house was built by a man named Will, who was then called away to fight in the Revolutionary War.

I'm pretty sure that prior to being served, my dinner was kept warm by a one-candlepower heat lamp that might have belonged to young Will himself. As in, a literal candle. I considered requesting that the marginally engaged server please reheat my food in ye olde microwave, but sensing he might spit some Virginia tobacco juice into my beurre blanc in revenge, I opted to shut up and eat.

The best part about waking at 4:45 the next morning was the realization that I did not, in fact, have food poisoning. Another hour's drive, this time back to Blacksburg, and we were ready to race. Our good weather fortune held from the previous day; once again it wasn't brutally humid. However, that positive mojo didn't completely hold where the course was concerned. The first few miles of drab roadway gave way to the leafy Huckleberry Trail, offering shade plus occasional musical entertainment. But we were back on the roads around Mile 10, where the scorching sun threatened to turn me into the same consistency as the state's celebrated Brunswick Stew. Although the final mile rose a modest 73 feet in elevation, it felt more like 730 under those conditions.

As soon as Kellie and I crossed the finish line in another sub-three-hour finish, my mission was to find the actual HokieBird mascot. They'd advertised that he'd be there; I was determined to pose for a photo. I'd avoided a photo op with overly handsy Bernie Brewer, the Milwaukee Brewers' mascot from my Wisconsin race, but the HokieBird was sort of special to me. Virginia Tech had been one of the competing teams when I'd attended the NCAA basketball tournament earlier in the year. While the HokieBird was no Peter the Anteater from UC Irvine (one of the all-time great sports mascots), he did have a certain something, and I kinda felt a little bond with him now.

Alas, the HokieBird had flown by the time we finished. I couldn't blame the poor human stuck inside that costume for blowing the coop under those conditions, but it was a letdown nonetheless. And that wasn't the sole bummer. Not only didn't I get that souvenir photo I'd hoped for, but I picked up the souvenir no one wants; a mild hamstring strain that would plague me for months to come.

New Hampshire

NEW HAMPSHIRE MARATHON (HALF), BRISTOL

"Woodah! Woodah heyah!"

The New Hampshire Marathon volunteer thrust a cup of "woodah" in my direction as I powered past the aid station. Instead of an exotic New England electrolyte drink, it turned out to be what Californians call "water." Accents weren't the only thing different around here; there was the temperature (brrrr!), the vivid tree foliage, and the intensely blue lakes that seemed to pop up around every corner.

I'd had plenty of opportunities to check out that landscape on my drive from Boston; a scheduled two-hour trip took well over four as what appeared to be half of Massachusetts' population traveled north for the weekend. The good news was that bibs and shirts could be picked up on race morning; the 9:00 a.m. start time afforded a rare opportunity to sleep a little later and even partake of the free hotel breakfast. It also meant I didn't have to panic about missing the start as I waited 15 minutes for my car windows to defrost, Hertz having failed to provide an ice scraper with my rental vehicle.

As with many things in New Hampshire, the race was small—about 400 participants. We half marathoners were bused to our starting point with plenty of time to spare, providing an opportunity for me to score some gossip about Madonna.

Yes, that Madonna.

After spotting a small group from the 50 States Half Marathon Club (made obvious by their club T-shirt and jackets), I joined them to share opinions on various races and how far along we were toward our goals (this was #39 for me). Annette mentioned she was from Michigan; Rochester, to be exact, close to where I grew up. I asked if

Gorgeous Newfound Lake, New Hampshire.

she'd known Adams High School's most famous grad. Oh yeah, she sure had.

"Madonna was very fun and popular," said Annette. "She was a cheerleader, very friendly. But when we came back to school for senior year, she had completely changed. She'd cut her hair, wore ragged thrift store clothes, and separated herself from everyone ... she became quite aloof. When she returned the next year for her sister's graduation, she stood up on a hill away from the rest of us, and that was the last time I saw Madonna."

I've always wondered if I unknowingly watched Madonna cheering when my high school's football team played Rochester Adams.... I'll never know, but it sure would be fun to tell people I had.

The course offered miles of autumnal scenic viewing around Newfound Lake, but it was a letdown when the final few miles hugged a busy road with narrow shoulders. Fast cars weren't all that went whizzing past. When an especially animated group of spectators

155

sent out a huge cheer in my direction, I smiled and granted them an appreciative wave ... right as the lead man in the full marathon sped past me. Embarrassment at accepting applause meant for someone else didn't teach me a lesson, however; I was tricked a few more times by stealthy marathoners overtaking me from behind before I finally crossed the finish line (to the applause of exactly no one).

My agenda for the day turned out to be overly ambitious for the limited time I had available. Locating a cider mill lost out to two priority items: visiting the setting for my all-time favorite novel and meeting a presidential candidate.

While *The Cheerleader* may sound rather lightweight, this fictionalized tale based on author Ruth Doan MacDougall's life as a 1950s teen in small-town New Hampshire is anything but. Thanks to what has become something of a cult following for the book, it wasn't too tough for my online research to yield info about the actual places that inspired MacDougall's work, so off to Laconia I went. The stand where she'd scooped ice cream at a summer job had closed for the season, but I found the Colonial Theater where main characters Snowy and Tom had their first date (it's not a YA novel, I promise!). Of course, I didn't expect 2019 Laconia to resemble 1950s Gunthwaite, but it was sad to see the once-grand theater in disrepair, the tattoo joints now doing business where Snowy had once shopped for prom dresses. Yet it was thrilling to stand on the same streets where the fictional teens of Gunthwaite had lived their lives; I absorbed my surroundings as best I could so that in my annual re-reading of *The Cheerleader* I'll be able to truly visualize those scenes. There was no time to linger in Laconia, though, as I was late for my next adventure.

In the year before a presidential election, candidates are as prevalent in New Hampshire as those ubiquitous cider mills I missed out on. As a political junkie, I had a lifelong dream of partaking in a bit of the retail politics that marks the early months of the campaign season. But on that particular day, many of the marquee names were elsewhere; the two Democrats around were Joe (who?) Sestak and spiritual advisor to the stars Marianne Williamson. That was an easy choice for me, especially because the Williamson happening promised to be Peak Marianne: a yoga class followed by a "Meditation on the Power of Peace." But by the time we would have meditated, levitated and whatever else, I wouldn't have made it to my next stop in Maine until midnight. So I settled on an event headlined by one of the few Republicans running—former Massachusetts governor Bill Weld.

Weld was speaking at Oktoberfest in Derry between 3 and 4 p.m.; when I arrived at 3:30 to find the tiny venue's parking lot full, I was directed to an impossible-to-locate overflow lot. Back to the venue for me, where the handful of now-open parking spots was a bad sign—Weld had probably finished speaking. Quickly tossing down my $12 entry fee, I realized this Oktoberfest was very New Hampshire–like in size; a few beer booths, a tent of craft vendors, and a bandstand. That stage where Weld had likely made his speech was now filled by a bluegrass band. Dang it!

While scanning the small crowd I spotted two young men in Weld T-shirts; standing with them was a woman chattering away at Weld himself. Seized by moxie born of adrenaline, I insinuated myself into the group as Random Woman blabbered on. When at last she paused for breath, Weld turned his attention to me; shaking his meaty paw, I told him that while I'm a California voter, I wanted to thank him for fighting the good fight. Random Woman resumed her monologue as I took

Bill Weld and me—yes, he really is that tall.

out my phone; one of the campaign staffers offered to take my photo with Weld.

After thanking Weld for the photo, I briefly wandered around the craft booths so I wouldn't appear to be a nutter who shows up alone at an Oktoberfest to stalk a presidential candidate (although that's apparently what I am). But Maine was calling and I had to answer. I missed out on that fresh New Hampshire cider, but I had a bottle of woodah for the drive to Maine, a new medal and T-shirt, plus the satisfaction of achieving a longstanding goal.

Maine

Maine Marathon (Half), Portland

In what was a banner year for one-hit wonders, in 1971, several musical acts exploded onto the scene only to fade quickly into oblivion. Who can forget Coven's counterculture classic "One Tin Soldier"? Then there was "Timothy," The Buoys' upbeat ditty about a mine explosion with undertones of cannibalism. A favorite of mine came courtesy of the Five Man Electrical Band. Their song "Signs," a protest against view-blocking, rule-posting signage by "the establishment," crossed my consciousness many times throughout my Maine Marathon experience. While none of the signs I encountered were blockin' out the scenery, a few had the potential for breakin' my mind (if only just a little).

Traveling on Maine's highways revealed a state awash in "Moose Crossing" signs. I hoped for a sighting … prayed to avoid colliding … neither situation materialized. Packet pickup was a pleasure, with race organizers offering the always-appreciated T-shirt size exchanges. Pickup was at the same University of Southern Maine location as the race start and finish. As much as I love a college campus, let's say the architecture here was no match for Bryn Mawr (an admittedly very high bar).

But this route was not about architecture; instead, it featured natural beauty in abundance. To experience all of that, we had to cross the start line, something that seemed in doubt when shortly before gun time the inflatable start line arch went *poof!* and collapsed into a massive plastic pile on the ground. Race officials hurriedly brought the behemoth back to life; we could only hope the thing wouldn't once again deflate and then clobber us as we passed below.

I targeted the pacer carrying the 3:00 half marathon sign as my motivational object for the race. This obsession wasn't about pace so much as about catching my afternoon flight out of Boston. Two days earlier my drive from Massachusetts to New Hampshire took twice as long as planned thanks to all of the traffic heading north for the weekend. How many of those returning Massholes (don't wag your finger at me, Ma Ingalls; this term appears in the Oxford English Dictionary) might prevent me from reaching Logan airport on time?

Making sure to keep the pacer behind me, I turned my attention to relishing the Ulster Scots influence along the course: a skirl of bagpipes to start the race, solo pipers scattered along the route playing their mournful tunes, and even step dancers doing their thing. The spirited crowd support featured signs that provided both humor and a dose of reality. A sign that reads, "You're almost there!" can be ironically humorous at Mile 1. A sign that reads, "You're almost there!" at Mile 9 is plain old cruel. The sign I most enjoyed this day was held by a young man standing several yards past the start that read, "Shit Ton of Miles to Go." Truth, my brother.

Soon the 3:00 pace sign passed me; as the pacer slowed to a walk, I passed her in return.

"My goal is to stay ahead of you," I told her. "Are you doing a run/walk?"

"Yeah, that's what I'll be doing the entire race," she replied. "Your pace looks great!"

Since she was run/walking the whole way, I knew not to freak out every time I saw that sign go by ... as long as the final pass was me overtaking her and not the reverse. Still, it can be maddening to play the pass-and-be-passed game with the folks who run/walk a race, as they alternate running segments with recuperative walking. When I've worked hard to pass someone, I have a psychological need for them to stay behind me. Hard as I tried, I could not shake the pacer for the better part of the race; it wasn't until around Mile 11 that I finally lost her for good.

As I approached the finish line, there was one more sign for me to contend with: two race officials stepped in front of me in the finish chute, unfurling a banner for a runner to break through in their moment of triumph. After the previous day's race where I reveled in applause meant for full marathoners coming up behind me, this time I figured out that yeah—this banner was not intended for me. Sure enough, shortly after I crossed the line, the first-place woman in the full marathon blasted through that banner in just under three hours.

On the drive back to Boston there were more moose crossing signs (but no collisions) and the expected plethora of Massholes on the Maine Turnpike, but I made it to Logan Airport in plenty of time. In a mere three weeks I'd be back at Logan, this time to experience not merely driving alongside but racing with the fine citizens of Massachusetts.

Massachusetts

CAPE COD MARATHON (HALF), FALMOUTH

I knew I'd been traveling too often when I walked onto the Hertz lot at Logan Airport and thought, "Hey, there's my car from a couple of weeks ago!" And so "my" white Ford Fiesta and I were off on yet another adventure through Boston's Friday afternoon rush hour, this time to Cape Cod. Southbound traffic was better than the northbound leaf-peeper disaster three weeks prior, allowing me to make it to the bustling expo before closing. Driving around Falmouth in the dark proved to be a bit of a challenge; multiple circuits were required before I finally located the sheltered entrance to the Captain's Manor Inn B&B. As it was past normal check-in hours, I'd been given an access code for the door plus instructions on how to find my room, where I was promised the door would be ajar, key on the bed.

The logistics had seemed intimidating, but the elegant inn immediately wrapped me in a welcoming embrace as I wove my way down corridors and up stairways to my room. Once the logistical stress abated, hunger came knocking. A short walk down Main Street brought me to a hopping joint called Estia that was crawling with Friday date-night couples and groups of laughing friends. When I indicated my unwillingness to wait 30 minutes for a table, the hostess suggested I look for a seat at the bar. At last—here was my opportunity to say to a guy, "Is this seat taken?" I'm sure that the poor man was terrified that I'd follow up with "Come here often?" or "What's your sign?" But instead of cheesy '70s pickup lines, I focused in appreciative silence on what was possibly the best Greek dinner I've ever eaten and then took a quick stroll through the preppy town before catching six hours of sleep.

The sky was late-autumn azure the next morning as about 1,500 runners and walkers took off in perfect race conditions. I never cease to be amazed at the number of people who run in tank tops and shorts in such relatively cool weather; one shirtless dude (who I later learned was an incredible 81 years old) stunned me not merely with the sight of his bared torso but by repeatedly grazing me with that exposed flesh as we jostled at the crowded start line. It's never a wise idea to start a race at your top speed, but I felt compelled to put a significant amount of space between the two of us.

There was still some fall color to see along the out-and-back course dotted with charming homes, views of Martha's Vineyard, and shimmering ponds. When I had plotted out a plan to earn my remaining states the previous year, I had hoped my Massachusetts race would be an urban experience in Boston, but it hadn't worked out schedule-wise. To my delight, Cape Cod was so appealing that I didn't feel at all pouty about missing out on Boston. But I did harbor one major concern about this race—it had a hard three-hour time limit. Lately, I'd been flirting with finishes right around the three-hour mark; exceeding that number could mean no official finish time, and that would mean a return trip to Massachusetts to make my 50-state journey official.

I didn't spot any pacers that could have helped me to keep on track, but the ideal weather and flat course (plus my efforts at half-naked geezer avoidance) equaled a fast pace, not to mention

161

Cape Cod residents embrace the race.

the motivation of a certain treat at the finish line. I still craved the cider donut I'd opted out of tracking down earlier in the month so I could free up time for stalking presidential candidates in New Hampshire. Today's race advertised cider donuts at the finish; I was determined to get my hands on one before the supply ran out.

Thus I developed a mantra for the final two miles: "ci-der-do-nut, ci-der-do-nut," a rhythmic chant that delivered me to the finish in 2:53:50—Shirtless Guy a good distance behind and donuts still in abundance. (It was delicious, but I'll stick with a glazed twist going forward.)

The B&B check-out time of 11:00 might have meant no shower for me; when I requested late check-out, I was told that the folks who had booked my room for the next night were arriving early so I'd need to vacate on time. However, the very kind innkeeper offered the use of their overflow room. Showering in something called an overflow room ... were we talking sewage overflow or what? It turned out to be a small bedroom with bath in the basement, far more than adequate for my purposes. Feeling like the scullery maid was fine with me if it meant being able to do some stretching exercises and clean myself up before taking off for my next destination.

That drive was not without drama, courtesy of the infamous rotaries of Massachusetts. We have rotaries (aka roundabouts or traffic circles) at home, but ours can't compare to the high-speed, multiple exit rotaries of the East Coast. One Masshole had almost crashed into me in a rotary the day before by cutting me off—although he did me a favor by forcing me onto the correct exit. But now Siri led me onto a rotary exit that looked nothing like any road I'd seen on the trip to Falmouth.

Suddenly several gun-toting men appeared as if from nowhere, angrily shouting while gesturing at me to stop. Heart pounding, I slammed on the Fiesta's brakes, making sure my hands were visible atop of the steering wheel. As one of the gunmen approached, I gingerly lowered the car window, hoping he wouldn't think I was reaching for a weapon.

"Um, I think my GPS must have led me astray," I managed to utter.

After he brusquely spat out directions for extricating myself from the situation, I peeled out as fast as I could. On the way out I noticed signs for a correctional facility; it didn't strike me as one of those Club Fed places where some Hollywood actress caught up in the college admissions scandal might enjoy a few weeks of "me time."

I was beyond thrilled to put Mashpee, Massachusetts, in the Fiesta's rear-view mirror and get on the right road to Vermont.

Vermont

Nor'witch Halloween Half'Witch, Norwich

It was the wettest of times, and if not the coldest of times, still downright wicked. Combined with relentless rain, the 40-degree temperatures in Norwich, Vermont, made Halloween Half'Witch the most miserable race weather-wise I've ever endured. The good news is that this small-town competition was not without its redeeming qualities.

Driving up from Cape Cod took about four hours, with a major slowdown occurring around Stoneham, Massachusetts, which I randomly remembered to be the hometown of legendary figure skater/knee whack victim Nancy Kerrigan. That presented me with the opportunity to channel my inner Nancy by shrieking, "Why? *Whyyy*?" at the stalled Saturday afternoon traffic as a way to vent my frustration. Much of this trip covered the same territory I'd traveled three weeks earlier for the New Hampshire Marathon, but this event took me farther north. I couldn't help but notice an ominous change in terrain; the transformation from hills to mountains signaled that the next day's course, featuring 1400 feet of climbing, would be quite a challenge.

Norwich is such a tiny town that it lacks much in the way of hotel space, so I was staying across the river near Dartmouth College in Hanover. At last, an opportunity to see an Ivy League campus! The collegiate atmosphere set a fitting mood for the weekend's highlight: reconnecting with Gail, my college roommate who was now a resident of Vermont. We caught up on gossip and reminisced about days of yore over dinner at Murphy's on the Green before strolling over to the legendary Green itself, the centerpiece of Dartmouth's campus. On this evening thousands of votive candles lined the sidewalks; in the middle, candles spelled out *Shanti*, the Sanskrit word for peace. This was Diwali, the Hindu festival of light; students clad in vibrant Indian garb were celebrating with the creation of a breathtaking blaze.

A few hours later and their celebration would have been extinguished by the steady rain that began overnight. A true friend indeed, Gail joined me in Norwich for the race's start the next morning at a small park in the middle of town. Shivering under that wet blanket of cold air, we huddled in a gazebo with a group of racers in a fruitless effort to protect ourselves from the elements. Gail hung in there uncomplainingly as we waited for the Half'Witch to get underway, then waved goodbye as I took off in a drizzle that soon turned to downpour. The bucolic small-town setting gave way to rolling country roads: the rustic barns and fields filled with autumn color were barely visible due to the increasingly ghastly weather conditions. As the course rose and fell, I was grateful for the extra exertion those hills required because it kept my heart rate elevated, generating additional heat. Soon I found myself completely alone, no one visible ahead of or behind me. I hoped I was still on the correct course—there weren't many course markers, but, then again, there weren't many opportunities to take a wrong turn.

By the time nine miles had passed, whatever novelty there was to power walking through the Vermont rain had dissipated; I was frozen, waterlogged, and all-around miserable. The one thing that perked me up was when the occasional car would pass, horn honking and headlights flashing as its occupants wildly applauded my efforts. Perhaps they thought it would be wise to humor me because seriously—who but a nutcase capable of God-only-knows-what would be out in those conditions?

After what felt more like six hours than three, I slogged across a wet field to the finish line. My reward was a unique Halloween-themed medal; a witch flying on a broomstick slider indicated which race distance had been achieved. Yes, some hearty souls were completing not a half, not a full, but a 50K race—30 miserably cold, rain-soaked miles. The friendly race organizers encouraged me to stay for pizza, but my singular desire was to get in my car,

Feeling lonely—and sodden—in Vermont.

crank the heat up full blast, and hustle back to my hotel room with its extended 2:00 p.m. checkout.

As it happened, I would need every bit of that extra time, in part to do battle with my saturated sports bra, a challenging item to remove under the best of circumstances. My icy claws, still immobilized by my hours in the cold, made it a virtual impossibility today.

166

Five solid minutes of removal effort resulted in a heart rate even higher than that caused by trekking the hills of Vermont. Pausing to catch my breath, I contemplated my options; they seemed fairly limited. I could hope for a magic fairy to show up with scissors. Was JogBra removal in the job description of hotel maintenance men? In desperation I gave the *teta* tourniquet one final yank; freed at last from its confines, I celebrated with a long, hot shower.

The drive back to Boston made it apparent that some states still don't require headlights to be turned on when windshield wipers are in use. Wet, windy weather continued the next day, prompting Alaska Airlines to add a Salt Lake City fuel pit stop onto what was supposed to be my direct flight home. But the pilot changed his mind mid-flight, announcing he was "99% sure we'd make it to San Francisco."

Well … wasn't that reassuring? I never dreamed I'd be so happy not to be a 1 percenter.

South Carolina

KIAWAH ISLAND MARATHON (HALF)

"It's a must-do!"

"My all-time favorite!"

"Save it for your 50th state!"

When asking my fellow racers which events they'd recommend, I learned there are as many opinions about what makes for a great destination race as there are people. Someone else's idea of a bucket list race that set them swooning might not be the same as mine; conversely, I give high marks to some competitions that are rarely mentioned. So while I was happy that the highly touted Kiawah Island Marathon worked well with my schedule, I knew better than to anticipate a blissed-out experience. A flat course near water might make many an athlete weak in the knees (not literally, of course) but isn't quite my thing.

With my expectations properly adjusted, my concerns centered around the requisite mid–December travel. Would flying be miserable in advance of the holidays? I was shocked to find so much available airport parking—even in the best of times I'm often relegated to the back 40. Another nice surprise: no Snowmageddon imperiling my Chicago connection as had been previously forecast.

My lucky transportation mojo deserted me upon arrival at Kiawah Island. Who knew that South Carolina suffers from the same plague of traffic rotaries that afflicts Massachusetts? Circling around in rainy darkness after missing my turn, I finally managed to locate the Andell Inn, set amid a village that resembled a Disney-esque take on Cape Cod (perhaps inspired by the nearby rotary). There was the obligatory Lilly Pulitzer store, the touristy sweet shops, the self-consciously chic fusion restaurants. I ignored them all. My mission was to hustle to the race expo. Mere seconds after depositing my suitcase in the hotel room, door slamming soundly shut behind me, I realized I'd offloaded not merely my luggage but my wallet as well. Doubly problematic: my one and only room key was in the wallet. So less than five minutes after checking in, I was back at the front desk.

"Believe it or not," I smiled sheepishly at the clerk, "I've already locked myself out."

"Oh, that happens more often than you'd think," she lied.

"I'm sure it doesn't, but it's kind of you to say that."

Once again in possession of wallet and key, once again misjudging a rotary, I picked up my race swag at the expo then made a stop at a food market. Arriving back at the Andell Inn now three-for-three on rotary errors, I purchased a bottle of overpriced water at the front desk.

"Could you please charge this to my room?"

"Sure, what's your room number?"

"472."

"This hotel has three floors."

"Oh, uh ... 274?"

Sigh. "Your last name?"

I feared she may have asked my name to file a report of a mentally addled guest; fortunately, she merely looked up my room number (247, by the way). Once I was in my room, the realization struck that during my outing, I'd neglected to obtain a utensil. Showing my

At home, I only have to worry about mountain lions. Not so in South Carolina.

face again at the front desk was not an option I wished to consider; thus I can report that it is difficult, yet not impossible, to eat Greek yogurt with a coffee stir stick.

Breakfast began at 5:30 the next morning to accommodate the many race participants staying at the inn. There was much discussion about the rain that had continued throughout the night, but the precipitation miraculously stopped at the precise moment a group of us made the short walk toward the shuttle buses to the start. Mingling with the 4,000 other competitors, I noticed the welcome arrival of that fizzy feeling of excitement I get from attending a true destination race.

As I suspected, this race wasn't inherently "me." But it was obvious the organization was top-notch: along the course (where homes sell for up to a gobsmacking $20 million) were steel drum bands, taiko drummers, stilt walkers, unicyclists, and flame jugglers among other assorted randomness. Exuberant crowds brandishing signs made the race seem to go faster; I saw one particularly motivating sign that I'm positive I've never before seen on a race course.

The shirt and medal from Kiawah Island receive a mixed score on my rating scale. The artwork featured South Carolina's famous Palmetto trees swathed in Christmas lights. I had tried as much as possible to avoid holiday-themed races on my 50-state journey, preferring medals that reflect the local area rather than a Turkey Trot or New Year's Race that can be held anywhere. So while the Christmas reference was unwelcome, the overall South Carolina vibe compensated for the holiday tie-in.

One more rotary mishap before leaving town and I was on my way to Atlanta for that weekend's race #2. That meant crossing through South Carolina on state highways with such fascinating sights as a sausage maker offering custom killing (I don't want to know) and Fat Boy's Deer Processing plus endless adult entertainment and dollar stores. A budgeting word to the wise—when you spend all of your money on custom-killed sausage and porn, apparently there's only enough left over to shop at deep-discount establishments.

Georgia

JEFF GALLOWAY 13.1,
ATLANTA

I knew upfront that at this Georgia race I would confront a foe who has bedeviled me for years. I didn't expect that I'd also battle Siri, Deep Throat, and the Real Housewives of Atlanta.

As my drive from South Carolina neared its conclusion with a gas stop outside Atlanta, I made a tactical error by neglecting to visit the restroom. One would think that a person with so much race experience would have learned never to pass up an opportunity to use the facilities. A few miles later, traffic ground to a halt due to an accident; while it is psychologically painful to be stopped so close to one's destination, it's physically torturous when faced with an increasingly desperate need for relief. The sun had slipped below the Atlanta skyline by the time I was finally on the move again, plunging the world outside my car into darkness. Conveying directions to me through my phone, Siri led me through a maze of downtown inter-state connections ... until she didn't. Oh, such an inauspicious time for her to develop navigational laryngitis. I missed my exit ... then another ... and another.

I yelled at my phone. "Siri, are you there?"

"Yes, I'm here."

"Siri, use your voice for navigation!"

"Okay."

But the miles continued to tick by with nary a word from Siri on which way to go. Taking a random exit, I pulled over to attempt some tech magic on the phone but to no avail. At least the map on the rental car's navigation screen gave me a rough idea of the W Hotel's location; I managed to bumble my way there to a much-delayed arrival.

Midtown Atlanta throbbed with Saturday night traffic, a signifi-cant portion of which blocked the hotel entrance. Previous visions of tossing the keys at the valet then running to the restroom van-ished, as limos disgorging a parade of women in killer gowns foiled my plan—it was as if the Real Housewives of Atlanta were hosting a massive holiday shindig. As I located a parking garage, my desperate physical discomfort soon turned to fear.

On Saturday evenings in San Francisco, parking spots are as hard to find as a political conservative. Yet here in the heart of Midtown, the garage contained shockingly few cars—was this place even open? With no time to locate alternatives, I grabbed a parking spot then my suitcase. Directly before me, a door with quick hotel access appeared ... yet opening that door required a room key, which I didn't yet have in my possession. No problem, I'd locate another exit ... if I could find one.

I scurried from aisle to aisle, unable to work my way out of there, until at last—a staircase!!! Dragging my luggage up to street level, I opened the door expecting to find (logically, it seemed to me) a street. Instead, I found myself in a dimly-lit hallway. The corridor became progressively creepier until turning into a construction zone; I began to envision "Woman's Body Found in Midtown Garage" headlines. All I knew at this point was that waterworks would soon begin, whether as tears from my eyes or ... ahem.

Descending to another floor, I careened around the vast emptiness; I would not have been surprised if at any second Deep Throat had appeared offering cryptic Watergate clues—but hey, at least he might have known the way out. Exits into various office buildings and coffee shops were locked tight. Suddenly ... could it be ... a restroom? Surely this door, too, would be locked—yet it opened to reveal the loveliest public facility I've seen this side of Nordstrom. This was possibly a mirage; in that case, there's a security camera somewhere with some damning videotape footage.

Exiting the restroom/mirage, I spotted signs of life—a couple dressed to party. Their destination was irrelevant; I would follow that Housewife in her Pucci pants to my hotel or my death. Opening an unlocked mystery door, the party pair led the way to the streets of Atlanta. At last, I made it to my hotel, my room, and a well-deserved room service dinner.

The next morning, I warmed up with a 10-minute walk to the start line in the crisp 45-degree air. Although bib pickup was not allowed on race morning, the organizers very kindly made an exception for me after I let them know I had no way to attend the previous day's expo. On this day I'd be facing down a nemesis of mine: race founder Jeff Galloway was a 1992 Olympian, the person who deserves the credit (or is it blame?) for developing the run/walk race method beloved by many competitors. Their pace, made up of run segments broken up by slow, recuperative walks, often equals my power walking pace—meaning I am constantly passing, then being passed by, the same folks. Galloway deserves all the credit in the world for devising a method that has paved the way for countless people to participate in races. Yet phones and watches are programmed to time each segment, and those disembodied electronic voices, bleeps, and bloops are an unwelcome companion in my part of the pack.

It's not surprising that a race produced by the guy who invented this plan would draw many of his acolytes. Indeed it did; the first few miles of the race sounded like I was inside a mobile ICU where all of the patients are simultaneously dying. When the field thinned out the bleeps and bloops became less noticeable, allowing me to appreciate the course's parks, trails, and neighborhoods that offered picture postcard views of Atlanta's skyline.

At the Piedmont Park finish, Galloway himself was there for a meet and greet with fans. I passed on the photo op, feeling it was

Yes, I do love a striking city skyline (such as Atlanta's).

wrong to act chummy with someone whose name I curse (in jest!) on a regular basis. But I will say he seemed like a great guy and he put on a very nice race; an interesting side note is that the top two overall finishers were women, something I don't recall from any previous race that wasn't a women-only event.

The cotton-poly long-sleeved race shirt wasn't going to be a winner with me given the fabric (I love a 100% polyester tech shirt), but worst of all was the fit; with its oddly high neck and weird cut through the body, it gave me a look reminiscent of Hans and Franz from *Saturday Night Live.* Hopefully, none of those Real Housewives ran this race; this fashion statement would deservedly have merited their scorn.

2020
Florida
Alabama
Mississippi
Virtual Races

Florida

MAINLY MARATHONS GULF COAST SERIES, PENSACOLA

Gasoline was cheap on the Gulf Coast. Like, $1.99 cheap, about half of what it cost at home in February 2020. With so many gas stations, seemingly one per person, it was tempting to speculate that the main activity around those parts must be to drive around aimlessly for hours, then refill the gas tank and do it again. But when you tire of that activity, what then?

Well, you mosey on over to Waffle House to load up your

tank—in this case, your stomach—with eggs, hash browns, and biscuits. Because my observation of the Gulf Coast led me to conclude that the one thing threatening to outnumber gas stations is Waffle House locations.

Kellie and I had traveled to the Gulf to knock out a few half marathons—three states in three days, to be exact. Thanks to wintertime flight delays, our drive from New Orleans to the Marriott in Spanish Fort, Alabama, located off the felicitously named Bass Pro Drive, was done in the dark; it wasn't until the next morning as we traveled on county highways over the state line to Pensacola, Florida, that we noted the profusion of (automobile) gas and (dietary) oil stops.

The sun began its rise amid clear skies as our race got underway. As a Mainly Marathons race, the trademark short course brought us back repeatedly to the one and only (lavishly catered) aid station. Out and back, we power walked the roads of Big Lagoon State Park, sharing greetings and positive affirmations with many familiar faces I recalled from the Mainly races I'd attended the previous summer. Mainly Marathons seems almost cult-like for some folks who devote so much of their time to traveling with the race caravan. They bring to mind the Deadheads who used to follow the Grateful Dead on tour. But the Mainly Marathons bunch is a healthy, happy crew that merely requires a reasonable entry fee, not your entire life savings, to join the fun.

The terrain may have been repetitive, but it gave Kellie and me a chance to get caught up without distraction on the latest developments in our lives. Most important, it allowed us to agree that a Waffle House meal would be a personal goal for the trip. Because let's be honest, what's a race without goals? Time goals, food goals ... they're all good.

For the first time ever, I declined a race T-shirt. Mainly Marathons uses a cotton-poly blend for their shirts; I knew that I'd wear it once then off to charity it would go. But I never turn down a medal, and this one was in their renowned style—a state-shaped medal that would connect in a long chain to the additional state medals we'd complete during this Gulf Coast series.

That next state? Alabama. After some A&I (Advil and ice), we

Florida sunrise through the trees. Photograph by Kellie Bernardez.

were ready for a little adventure before race #2 of three the following day.

Alabama

MAINLY MARATHONS GULF COAST SERIES, SPANISH FORT

Mobile, Alabama, lays claim to hosting the first Mardi Gras parade in the United States. Who knew? I didn't, until I traveled there.

2. 50 States and Washington, D.C.

Following that morning's Florida race, Kellie and I drove to Mobile for lunch at the delightful Spot of Tea. We were amazed at how attractive the city is ... and here I will confess that Mobile is not a place I'd ever considered to be a tourist destination. Yet it resembles a scaled-down, cleaner New Orleans and during our visit was festooned everywhere with seasonally appropriate purple, green, and gold decor. Departing the restaurant (where I was called ma'am roughly a hundred times, something I always appreciate during visits to the South), we noticed there was some kind of police action taking place. My first suspicion was something big-city scary; instead, it was in preparation for the first parade of Mardi Gras season. Were we going to leave town without seeing that parade? Oh no, we were not.

It was worth a little wait. From our spot on the front row, we were assaulted (in a nice way) with waves of goodies thrown from floats; best of all we didn't even have to show *our* goodies to get them. We understood then why several spectators had arrived at the parade with enormous empty bags—they knew there was a mind-boggling amount of loot to be hauled away. In a half-hour or so, we amassed more than we could possibly carry away with us. Moon Pies, candies, sunglasses, cookies, beads galore, and that most random of items ... a package of Top Ramen. And you best believe I schlepped that ramen home to California, whereupon it became my husband's dinner with the addition of scallions, carrots, and spinach.

Grudgingly we tore ourselves away from the festivities to take some time off our feet in advance of racing the next morning. It turned out to be a typical Mainly Marathons experience that featured seven out-and-back laps through a park, this one covering Civil War battleground territory at Blakeley State Park in Spanish Fort. It wasn't difficult to envision regiments of soldiers dashing around the fields and woods brandishing their muskets. Here once again I learned that I don't always have the kind of race I expect. My anticipated crawl to the finish in Ohio's heat and humidity ended with a near–PR; on the other hand, I was unexpectedly speedy in sub-freezing Tulsa. On this perfect weather day in pancake-flat Alabama, I notched a new all-time slowest half marathon for no apparent reason.

As usual, one of my mental coping mechanisms on this repeated loop course was to fantasize about the snacks I'd select each time we completed a lap. Whatever shyness I had felt at my first few Mainly Marathons races about taking full advantage of the copious food and beverage offerings had long since vanished. Today's presentation exceeded even the typically bountiful Mainly Marathons spread due to the addition of King Cake, a delicacy available strictly during Mardi Gras season. I kept alive my years-long streak of missing out on the piece with the baby inside; I realize that any reader unfamiliar with King Cake will find this comment somewhere between puzzling and horrifying.

That King Cake was glazed pastry perfection; perhaps there is a credible reason for that all-time slowest finish after all. But we knew better than to overindulge. Kellie and I had a date with restaurant destiny coming up after the race while on the road to Mississippi. For this would be the day on which we would achieve our weekend goal...

...dining at Waffle House.

Mississippi

MAINLY MARATHONS GULF COAST SERIES, GULFPORT

Craving some greasy goodness, a little hangover food *par excellence*? If you're participating in the Gulf Coast Series, you're in luck! You could easily convince me that every single one of Waffle House's 2,100 locations is concentrated within the narrow corridor that Kellie and I drove on our adventure to the Gulf. Do you suffer from *feng shui* issues that require doors to face in certain directions? You can choose from among several locations positioned whichever way you want. Perhaps you desire certain window exposures to enhance your glowing complexion; there's sure to be a Waffle House nearby that meets those needs.

We needed a bare minimum of primping after our Alabama race, as the restaurant's atmosphere was the epitome of come-as-you-are. Indeed, the booth next to ours was inhabited by a gentleman of the vagrant bum persuasion. The entirety of my Waffle House knowledge to that point had come from news accounts of midnight brawls, so this mild-mannered gent was an improvement over the clientele we might possibly have encountered.

My three-item combo was delivered in segments roughly 10 minutes apart, appearing only as a result of repeatedly prompting our waiter. Thus I had sufficient time to evaluate the artery-clogging capacity of each portion of my meal. The eggs, hash browns, and grilled biscuit all made serious bids for the Oiliest Item award; Kellie's waffle not so much, but also it was not so outstanding as to merit an entire chain being named in its honor. I passed on snapping any food photos as I feared my phone might slip from my hand, dying a greasy death upon the floor like so many Waffle House patrons who had come and gone before. The verdict: In the hotly contested battle for biscuit supremacy, Bojangles takes the gold over Cracker Barrel, with Waffle House rounding out the podium.

I was touched by a conversation I overheard between the waiter and the residence-challenged gentleman in the adjacent booth. Approaching the man as he slumped over his coffee cup, the waiter said, "We can offer you a breakfast of eggs with toast or biscuits; which would you prefer, and how would you like your eggs?" Waffle House was not only giving the man a free meal but even offering him options. I imagine that being asked about his food preferences is something he doesn't often encounter. I know from past experiences volunteering at charity kitchens that choices are rarely available; offering them when possible is seen as a way to give the clients some sense of agency. You go, Waffle House. Nice job.

After bidding Waffle House *adieu*, Kellie and I were off to Gulfport, which felt like a short drive after the many miles we'd covered the first two days. That gave us time to quickly check out the grounds of Beauvoir, also known as the Jefferson Davis Home; this was the final residence of the president of the Confederacy. There was no time to linger, however, as we had a dinner date with my mother-in-law at an Italian place called Salute. I was greatly amused when Miss Betsy, with an audible gasp, recoiled in horror upon learning where our previous meal had been consumed. Catching up

Mainly Marathons' clever connecting medals. Photograph by Kellie Bernardez.

on family news was a nice prelude to our third race in three days the next morning.

Our course for Race #3 was situated on the Gulfport beach boardwalk. The weather was quite sultry, but a fortuitous breeze off the water made the humidity somewhat tolerable; unfortunately, the boardwalk was made of concrete, and my calves let it be known that they were not appreciative of the unforgiving surface.

Something else that made the day tolerable was our Tater Tot Hot Dish breakfast. I'd recently learned of this Minnesota specialty via the *New York Times*; erstwhile presidential candidate Senator Amy Klobuchar was said to have served her very own recipe at Iowa caucus house parties. The Minnesota brothers who run the Mainly Marathons series offer this as part of their rotating menu of food station staples. While not exactly comparable to a green smoothie or kale salad, after Waffle House it seemed downright healthy.

My food fest continued right up until the trip's end. After Kellie and I parted ways at the New Orleans airport, I discovered that the terminal featured its very own Café du Monde. By now, there was no pretending this trip was anything but a junk food fest of historic proportions, so I snagged a bag of three beignets. Along with hauling home MoonPies and Top Ramen from the mean streets of Mobile, I brought two of the three beignets back to the family for their enjoyment. Nothing brought back fond memories of that trip for the next month or so more than opening my purse, only to be assaulted by remnants of powdered sugar wafting about.

Virtual Races

It helps to go through life as a pessimist. Every time I'd been asked, "When do you finish your 50th state?" I'd reply, "Well, assuming everything goes according to plan, it should be May of 2020 in West Virginia." That would be met with laughter and "Oh, I'm sure it'll all work out! You'll get it done!"

Well, optimists of the world, allow me to refer you to that notorious ruiner of plans, the Global Pandemic. Thanks to Covid-19 I didn't make it to West Virginia in May, or for that matter to Rhode Island and Connecticut the month before. In March of 2020, my home state of California went into lockdown mode with most of the country soon following suit. I can't shed too many tears when comparing my situation to that of so many others, but I'll admit to feeling a little bummed out when I canceled the gathering I'd planned for that final race in West Virginia. There would be no festive flight to the Greenbrier Resort with Todd, Isabel, and her husband Mark; no meeting up with Kellie (arriving from Montana) and Lori (Michigan) for a weekend of mimosas and massages—although I suspect that in Mark's case, the Greenbrier's golf courses held as least as much allure as celebrating my milestone.

Instead of swanky spa treatments and gourmet meals, the month of May found me cutting my own hair and hoarding canned beans. I was stuck at 47 states as race after race was called off throughout the spring ... and the summer. Keeping up my mileage was important; I needed to stay race-ready for whenever normal life resumed. But I could sense the temptation to shift into low maintenance mode, which would mean facing a huge re-training curve—or being completely unprepared should a race be given the green light.

That opened the door to something I had long avoided: the virtual race. There are plenty of them out there. Some require proof of having run a specified distance on your own before mailing out a medal and shirt; others are more than happy to ship the goodies without seeming to care if you do the miles or not. It felt equivalent to buying a medal; in the Before Times, I had no incentive to participate. Perhaps if I lived in an area with no races available ... say, a remote Alaskan fishing village ... I could see the appeal. (Although if I lived in a remote Alaskan fishing village my energy would be directed toward moving elsewhere, not running half marathons.) Plus—and this is a key point—virtual races don't count toward 50-state half marathon totals, the goal that I was working toward.

With the onset of the pandemic, race directors were stuck with medals and shirts that would have gone into the garbage bin unless the races were converted to virtual events; that's what happened with the April race I had registered to power walk in Newport, Rhode Island. Suddenly the idea of churning out 13.1 miles in exchange for a shirt and medal seemed like it might, given the circumstances, be okay. I'd get my training miles and a shirt I'd earned the right to wear—although hopefully, no one would ask me how I'd liked Newport because who knew when, if ever, I'd be able to answer that question?

That's how my grumpy self ended up toeing an imaginary start line on the Iron Horse Trail at 7:00 a.m. on Easter Sunday. There was no way to mistake the sunburned grasses of San Ramon, California, for coastal Newport, but since I hadn't ventured outside my neighborhood for several weeks, even this familiar trail felt a little alien. My pandemic running gear was alien, too; I don't normally wear a neck gaiter in mild weather, but when pulled up over my nose it made for a decent face mask (in a Mort from Bazooka Joe kind of way).

I hoped that people who might otherwise be outside would stay home to enjoy chocolate from the Easter Bunny. Or maybe they'd be indulging in that wine everyone was drinking for breakfast while tending to their sourdough starter if the Covid-19 memes were to be believed. But the paths were more populated than I expected. A handful of folks sported face masks, but the majority seemed unconcerned about all things viral. While most were reasonably good about keeping six feet of distance there were notable exceptions; even pointedly moving off the path into the surrounding foot-high grasses while glaring from above my Mort-mask didn't elicit much reaction.

Crabby though I might have felt about virtual racing, it did turn out to be an effective motivator. As a bonus, it gave me an excuse to visit my favorite bagel place for a little indulgence—take out, of course, no dining-in allowed. It's important to replicate the race day experience as much as possible, and that means permission to loosen a few dietary restrictions.

Oh, who am I kidding? By this time, my dietary restrictions had been discarded as quickly and carelessly as those masks and gloves people were leaving all over the place.

Knowing it would be a while before real racing resumed, I made a plan to complete one virtual half marathon per month lest I emerge from lockdown twice as big and half as fast. Virtual racing couldn't replace the excitement of a start line thrumming with competitors ready to race, the visual stimulation of a new course, or the thrill of a medal being placed around my neck at the finish. But it added a little fun to a very un-fun situation. I didn't mind paying for those shirts and medals because I knew that race directors were suffering significant financial losses due to cancelations. I wanted to do what little I could to help ensure that when we emerged from the pandemic there would still be races to attend.

By the way, remember that sneak-preview race shirt I'd lusted after at Run the Bluegrass in Kentucky? The 2020 edition of the race ended up with a virtual option thanks to Covid-19; you'd better believe I signed up right away. That long-sleeved checkerboard beauty belongs to me now, one of the few bright spots resulting from dreadful circumstances.

As summer dragged on, whatever excitement I'd felt about virtual races dried up and died like the vegetation around drought-stricken California. I continued cranking out a half marathon per month, less from internal motivation, more from the fact that so many non-refundable events for which I had optimistically registered converted into virtual-only races.

With August came the miracle of real-live races in both West Virginia and Rhode Island with social distancing rules firmly in place; start times were staggered with participants kept safely separated. I wasn't worried about catching cooties during a race, but what about the flights to get there and back? I'm no spring chicken; hell, I'm not even a summer chicken anymore. Temptation also presented itself in the form of November races in Rhode Island and Connecticut scheduled a week apart; by staying out east for 10 days I'd earn two states with one round trip. But in the end, I couldn't justify the risk of viral exposure from airplanes, airports, and fellow travelers (aka mobile disease vectors) or shake the specter of falling ill on a solo trip with no way to get back home.

This was my new reality; I decided there was no way I'd board an airplane until the health crisis was well under control. With that day unlikely to arrive for some time, virtual half marathons now represented more than training motivation. No, they didn't count toward my 50-state club award, and yes, I'd still travel to complete those states in person when I could. In the meantime, virtual races from those final three states would serve as placeholders, providing a sense of accomplishment as I persevered through the pandemic.

Then came the fires. August's freak dry-lightning storm sent a massive bolt between my house and Isabel's next door. Fortunately, our homes and families emerged mostly unscathed; only a handful of electrical items were fried. The same could not be said for my 40' redwood tree, a hawk, and a family of squirrels who met untimely deaths via thunderbolt. Our cars were hurriedly packed with treasured objects in anticipation of evacuation; soon our town was surrounded by a ring of fire that greedily consumed the desiccated terrain. We can never repay the debt we owe to the firefighters who saved us from the same fate as our flora and fauna.

How to cope with living in a state that's on fire? My go-to stress reducer is, of course, exercise, but week after week of toxic, ash-filled air stole one of the few joys left untouched by Covid-19. Checking the Air Quality Index became a new compulsion as I played an unhealthy guessing game, calculating how much was too much gunk to risk inhaling. As much as I craved a good power walk, many days it would have been healthier to sit on my couch chain-smoking a carton of cigarettes. Unbreathable air, a pandemic, caught between sheltering in place or evacuating ... the old version of me wouldn't have recognized the world I was now living in. Somehow I had become my own Ma Ingalls.

When the air quality allowed, I managed not one but two West Virginia virtual halfs. As with regular races, the virtual kind are not without their challenges; witness September's Greenbrier River Trail virtual half, when I suffered a bee sting to my groin area shortly before I reached Mile 4. (Of course, this was 2020, so it might have been a murder hornet that attacked me.) It marked at least the third time I've been stung while power walking. Friends say it must be because I smell so sweet but trust me: I know how I smell when I'm power walking on a hot summer day, and sweet it ain't.

Although my physical reaction to being stung is unpleasant (in this case an itchy swelling several inches in diameter) it doesn't require immediate medical help; good thing, because one drawback of virtual races is the lack of medical staff on-site. Another drawback?

185

No water stations. My preferred trail for longer power walks includes a few drinking fountains, but now they were swathed in don't-touch-this plastic. Some people swear by hydration belts, those devices that allow athletes to carry a bottle or four of fluid during exercise, but I've never liked the idea of sloshing while I power walk. Whether battling thirst or bee stings, in a virtual race you're forced to either come prepared or tough it out.

The fires raged on into autumn, time for the Hartford Marathon, the race marking my kinda-sorta 50th and final state. The organizers requested that participants complete their run or walk between October 8 and 11. Whether that would mean an unseasonably early deluge of rain or an Indian summer heatwave, the weather wasn't a concern; by now I knew I could handle anything. My single worry was that "Spare the Air" alerts were being issued daily due to the continued poor air quality. When I awoke before sunrise on October 10 to discover that the air had inexplicably cleared overnight, I quickly pulled on my power walking gear then headed out for Hartford...

...Hartford Road in Danville, California, that is. So determined was I to give this race some connection to the real deal that I'd scoured online maps seeking anything named Hartford—a city, a street, a park, it didn't matter—to incorporate into my virtual course. As it turned out I didn't have to venture too far from home; Hartford Road crossed the same Iron Horse Trail I'd used for all my virtual races, a few miles farther north than the section I'd been regularly navigating. As an atmospheric bonus, this part of the trail featured miles of tree canopy arching over the path; with some imagination those oaks and redwoods became maples and hemlocks, giving my morning a little New England flavor. The air may not have had the crisp feel of a Connecticut autumn, but breathing clean air for the first time in such a very, very long time was enough to make me ecstatic.

Returning to Hartford Road after the race to snap a photo of my medal, a couple approached me as they ran up the trail. "Nice medal," said the man, "what race is that from?" I explained the Hartford connection, adding, "It's a little cheesy, I know, but why not?" We all laughed as they continued on their run, calling out,

Proof that I ran Hartford (if not in it, at least *on* it).

"Congratulations!" I appreciated that the race organizers had sent the medal and shirt in advance so that I could enjoy my swag right away; receiving congratulations from strangers made my virtual race feel a little bit more like the real thing.

Even with the kudos and the bling, though, there's simply no substitute for a race. I'm proud of the fact that in the face of extraordinary circumstances I persevered, creating new goals and methods of motivating myself. I'm also proud that I didn't give in to the temptation to take actions I felt uncomfortable with purely to meet a predetermined time schedule. I had no doubt that I'd finish up those final three states in person, but I'd do it when I could truly immerse myself in the experience, free from worry (except for those scary mini-planes; I'll always worry about those).

Not only that, but I wouldn't stop there.

You see, my running club also has a 100 half marathons challenge. Once I completed those final three states, I'd have 87 lifetime half marathons. That means if I complete 13 additional half marathons (anywhere in the world, including close to home) I'll score 13 more medals, 13 more race T-shirts, and make more wonderful memories … but every bit as important, I'll maintain the fitness that's crucial for keeping all of life's goals and adventures within walking distance.

* * *

The 50-state challenge is complete!

When the Covid pandemic eased somewhat in the spring of 2021, the time had arrived to wrap up my 50-state adventure. An epic round trip across America via Amtrak train provided a once-in-a-lifetime solution to my air travel aversion. During that 16-day trek, I completed half marathons in West Virginia, Connecticut, and finally in Rhode Island—coincidentally at the Newport Rhode Race, my original pandemic-inspired virtual half. (I can now state with authority that Newport is just as lovely as advertised, should anyone inquire when they see my race shirt.) The events were scaled back to accommodate health concerns, but that couldn't put a damper on my euphoria. Arms raised in joyous triumph, I crossed the finish line in Newport amid a spray of champagne and cheers from members of the 50 States Half Marathon Club.

Was the 50-state challenge worth the effort? Definitively yes. And as fulfilling as achieving that goal feels, the best part by far was the step-by-step journey to get there.

3

References

Film Reviews, Book Reviews and Power Walking Resources

Rest, and plenty of it, is an important component of any training plan. Bodies need time to rebuild the muscle that exercise tears down; our brains need a break, too. That means not only getting adequate sleep but taking time to get off your feet and relax—and that means giving yourself permission to indulge in some movie watching or allowing yourself to get lost in an absorbing book.

Six Flicks That Will Inspire You to Perspire

Here's a look at some documentaries and fictional films that provide not just entertainment but also insights into racing that apply to both running and power walking.

A Long Run (2014)

Runner's World magazine has served as the bible of road and trail runners (and yes, power walkers, too) for decades. The driving force behind the creation and expansion of the magazine was Bob Anderson; viewers will not be surprised to learn that Anderson has himself been a devoted runner since the age of 14. *A Long Run* toggles between Anderson's history in the worlds of sports and publishing with his 2012 mission to mark his 50th-year running anniversary in epic fashion. His goal? To run 50 races of varying distances during that calendar year, 350 miles in total, at an overall average sub–7:00 per mile pace.

The film puts forth a hypothesis I am finding to be fact: that age has a greater effect on recovery than it has on performance. Anderson is able to maintain his goal pace for most of his races but competing in all of those events so close together makes overcoming injuries a significant challenge. We witness Anderson receiving physical therapy treatments, we watch as he applies kinesiology tape ... all of the things that runners and power walkers do to keep mobile, especially as we age. Throughout the film it's fun to see the little things that when added up, create the racing experience; it shows us not merely the training but day-of-race moments like lining up for the shuttle bus to the start line, pinning on a race bib, even struggling to open a bottle of electrolyte fluid after a race.

A Long Run Rating: Five Energy Gels

Brittany Runs a Marathon (2019)

While viewing this amiable comedy about a hard-partying, overweight young woman who decides to train for the New York City Marathon, I expected to receive the usual dollop of Millennial gross-out humor served up with a big helping of single-gal-in-her-20s references on the side. Knowing it was highly rated, and given the relative lack of films about running (compared to, say, the ubiquitous superhero flicks), I figured it might be worthwhile to wade through the less relatable parts to find whatever bits there might be about race training. *Brittany Runs a Marathon* turned out to be far more nuanced and emotionally involving than I'd anticipated, a realistic drama wrapped up in comedic clothing.

While the titular character's story arc bears some similarity to the protagonist in the film *Bridesmaids*, *Brittany*'s more poignant approach allows Jillian Bell to create a character I wanted to hug and then sit down for a stern lecture. In truth she probably hit a little too close to home; I, too, have self-sabotaged my never-ending trudge toward healthy habits more times than I care to remember. To Bell's (and writer Paul Downs Colaizzo's) credit, Brittany is allowed the latitude to be unlikeable at times as she runs (and stumbles) along the metaphorical road to becoming the person she strives to be. Colaizzo is said to have based the story on a friend's actual experience, which may in part account for the realistic feel of the writing and acting.

It's hard to imagine anyone not enjoying this movie simply because they aren't a runner; that's not at its core what *Brittany* is all about. But my personal experience with training for full marathons and with racing in New York City undoubtedly added to my enjoyment. I could quibble about the accuracy of a few details—for example, the entry lottery doesn't occur so close to race day—but in no way did that stop me from being completely compelled by the story.

Brittany Runs a Marathon Rating: Five running shoes

Free to Run (2016)

The foundations of modern running are explored in this documentary with its central hypothesis that running is both free and freeing, that even though it has evolved into a big business, it still comes down to two crucial things—an athlete and a pair of shoes.

It leads off with historical (and, to me, hysterical) footage of runners from decades ago, and the accompanying commentary underscores how much things have changed: Physicians pontificate about runners risking their lives by participating in the sport; hands are wrung over women runners causing themselves harm due to a supposed excess of both body fat and emotion. Running icons such as Kathrine Switzer, Bobbi Gibb, and Frank Shorter give a glimpse into how the highly regulated amateur running atmosphere in the '60s and '70s gave way to the sport of today—in great part thanks to the advocacy work of legendary runner Steve Prefontaine.

Running as a social phenomenon is explored as the film progresses through the boom of the 1980s and the subsequent commercialization of the sport. But always at the heart of the film is the elemental beauty of running. While the documentary has a somewhat New York City–centric lens, that's not a bad place to anchor this story that shows how hard work on the part of the sport's pioneers created the running community that exists today.

Free to Run Rating: Five Clif Bars

From Fat to Finish Line (2015)

Fat, for some folks, is an emotionally charged word. But given that it's part of this documentary's title and freely used by the people it profiles, I assume the participants are okay with it. The dozen runners we meet in *From Fat to Finish Line* have a clear-eyed perspective on their weight loss journey, addressing both the circumstances that caused them to become overweight and the role that exercise has played in their successful weight loss. I was surprised to find my eyes welling up with tears several times while watching this movie; every single story felt amazingly inspirational.

The 197-mile Florida Keys Ragnar serves as the framework for the film; it's one in a series of overnight team relay races held in scenic locations. The featured team came together via online connections that were made during their weight loss endeavors; each member had independently made the discovery that running was key to their weight loss success and to maintaining their new way of life. Throughout their Ragnar adventure, the runners reflect back on where they started—most of them having lost around 100 pounds. While they are not what some people would consider athletes, as *Runner's World* editor in chief David Willey states, "The sport is big enough for everybody." That's key to what so many people appreciate about the running and power walking community; that climate of inclusivity and supportiveness is on full display here.

I've never been tempted to participate in a Ragnar, but after watching the first portion of the film and witnessing the camaraderie between teammates, I began to think maybe I'd like to give one a try. But then reality set in as the participants struggled through the overnight portion of the race, battling cramps, gastrointestinal issues, and even the specter of alligators; at this point, I decided "hmmm, maybe my first impression was correct after all." Director Angela Lee gives the viewer a good feel for what the Ragnar experience is all about. I was touched by the human kindness that these 12 people displayed and have the utmost respect for their journeys toward healthy living as well as their journey to the Ragnar finish line.

From Fat to Finish Line Rating: Five finisher medals

McFarland USA (2015)

I've never been involved in the sport of cross-country running, nor have I lived in an agricultural community. But I felt I had a better understanding of both after viewing *McFarland, USA*. Best of all, this film, based on a true story, is truly enjoyable entertainment—even my son who doesn't particularly care for movies or for running absolutely loved it. Kevin Costner stars as schoolteacher Jim White. "Blanco," as the students call him, creates a high school cross-country team from scratch in a small San Joaquin Valley town, learning about the sport from guidebooks at the same time he's coaching the kids. In the meantime, he's also getting an education as to what life is like for the students and their families and the harsh realities of agricultural fieldwork.

Although *McFarland, USA* may bear some similarities to classic sports movies like *Hoosiers* or *Breaking Away*, this didn't feel like a formulaic retread. The acting, setting, and, yes, the running, make *McFarland* a film that's worth watching—in my case, more than once.

Bonus! In 2016, the City of McFarland began hosting an annual half marathon; the course takes participants past many of the film's locations and the field of participants has even included runners whose stories were featured in the movie. I had planned to power walk the race in 2020 until it became yet another cancelation due to Covid-19. Hopefully, the event will continue in subsequent years; if it does, you'll find me there.

McFarland, USA Rating: Five tech T-shirts

Skid Row Marathon (2017)

A Los Angeles judge, himself a passionate runner, develops a program on that city's Skid Row to encourage men and women of the Midnight Mission to find fitness, friendship, and a sense of worth through running. *Skid Row Marathon* relates the story of superior court judge Craig Mitchell as he reaches out to people struggling with substance abuse, criminal backgrounds, and homelessness. Mitchell offers them an opportunity to gain confidence and improve their health through positive life choices, centered on involvement in a running program. With a marathon as their goal, the Mission residents discover not only the physical benefits of running but also indirect benefits such as self-esteem and self-confidence.

Their journey is not without its setbacks; writer/director Mark Hayes documents the story of each participant with sympathy that's grounded in reality. Hayes doesn't sugar-coat the runners' stories or their struggles with the arduous task of turning their lives around. This documentary does an excellent job of illustrating how Mitchell's program benefits participants during their training process (the commitment and goal setting required) and then again via the satisfaction of having achieved their goal. It's also inspiring to witness the selflessness of someone like Judge Mitchell who gives freely of his time to make a difference within his community.

Skid Row Marathon Rating: Five race bibs

Some of us grew up in an era when runners and competitive walkers were considered oddballs; perhaps our families didn't support our athletic ambitions. We might struggle with our weight or our health, either mental or physical. We all bring different sets of life experiences to our sport. These films are a powerful reminder that running and power walking can play a major role in bringing out the best in those of us who are willing to lace up a pair of shoes and hit the road or trail.

A Dozen Books That'll Get You Up and Walking

Looking for a book that will make you laugh, cry, or even become a better athlete? Here are a few to consider. You'll find practical guides that can help you to develop a power walking training plan, whether for general recreation, overall fitness, or race training. Others are memoirs covering a wide range of viewpoints and stories from the most laid back of run-walkers to the elite athletes who paved the path for today's racing environment. All of them are in their own way insightful, educational, or just plain fun.

Training Plans

Beginner's Guide to Power Walking
  by Janice Meakin (Barron's, 2003)

At 96 pages, Meakin's book is a quick and easy way to access solid information on power walking training plans. It begins with basic information on topics such as stretching exercises, and the heart of Meakin's book is the training programs she details for varying fitness levels. She addresses the needs of everyone from the complete beginner aiming to become active to a full marathon walking plan, and even includes guidelines for someone undertaking advanced level week-long trekking. Utilizing simple, colorful charts, Meakin provides concise day-to-day and weekly workouts in an easy-to-follow format.

The Complete Guide to Marathon Walking
  by Dave McGovern (Echo Point Books & Media, 2016)

So you think you might want to walk a full marathon? That's a great idea! I've power walked three of them and I can vouch for the fact that both the training and the races themselves are life-changing experiences. McGovern has coached countless walkers to complete a full marathon; in this book, he shares his how-to's in a friendly, accessible style. Along with taking a deep dive into stretching exercises and walking techniques, he also addresses the subject of fundraising races. That's something I haven't become involved with, but for many people the decision to join up with an organization such as Team in Training or an individual commitment to raise funds for a charity can be a powerful motivator for race participation.

McGovern's in-depth look at all aspects of the marathon training experience for walkers is an invaluable resource that goes beyond what's covered in Meakin's book; save this one for when you've mastered the basics and feel ready to mentally and emotionally commit to a full 26.2 miles of marathon power walking.

Memoirs, Motivation, and More

Born to Run: A Hidden Tribe, Superathletes,
and the Greatest Race the World Has Never Seen
by Christopher McDougall (Knopf, 2011)

McDougall takes his readers on an unforgettable voyage to Mexico where we meet the Tarahumara Indians of the Copper Canyons, superstar runners from a reclusive tribe who thrive in a remote and deadly area. There, the author takes part in a race featuring a fascinating band of American characters who travel to Mexico to take on the challenge of competing against the Tarahumara. This book strips running down to the elemental aspects of the human body versus nature, versus physical limitation, and versus the mind, while also relating an absorbing tale of strikingly different cultures and personalities that are brought together by a common bond.

Confessions of an Unlikely Runner
by Dana Ayers (GP Press, 2017)

Dana Ayers' book *Confessions of an Unlikely Runner* is a slim volume in which she shares her experience as a non-athletic type who participates in running-related sporting events. Portraying herself as a sort of "everywoman," she sums up her early athletic background, eventual involvement with running as an adult, and the varied types of competitions in which she has participated. She finishes up with cross-training and motivational tips.

Ayers comes across as someone it would be fun to befriend and take part in races with. Her best work is when she allows a scene to speak for itself, such as a 2 a.m. meal break on a "cow farm" during a 24-hour race. Also enjoyable are Ayers' descriptions of less common contests such as a Tough Mudder obstacle course and a Ragnar relay race. The book reaches an emotional high point when telling the story of a Tennessee-to-Boston fundraising relay that benefited bombing victims of the 2013 Boston Marathon. Ayers provides solid insights into why racing can be fun and motivating, particularly for back-of-the-pack runners and power walkers.

The Long Run: A Memoir of Loss and Life in Motion
by Catriona Menzies-Pike (Crown, 2017)

A young Australian woman whose parents lost their lives in a plane crash carries on with her life, eventually finding herself at loose ends. While on a trip to India, she randomly declares that she will train to run a marathon. Catriona Menzies-Pike's book is part memoir, part feminist cultural critique, part women's running history. The heart of the work is the transformative power of both grief and running and how the sport has been portrayed as it applies to women throughout history. It's a unique take on the running memoir, lifting it beyond the usual boundaries into something literate, thought-provoking, and utterly engaging. When an introduction name-checks Gertrude Stein, David Foster Wallace, and the *Stuff White People Like* website, you know this will be an eclectic, literate work of singular style.

While the theme of personal pain underlies the story, the focus here is on sport itself. Throughout her memoir, Menzies-Pike threads an ongoing analytical discourse on what running has represented to women historically and what it means to her in the present and also her view of running as a feminist, cultural, and personal statement. My favorite moment in the book occurs in the closing chapters when Menzies-Pike arrives in America to run the New York City Marathon, the culmination of that randomly conjured goal from years earlier. When she has an opportunity to meet Kathrine Switzer, Menzies-Pike confesses she is starstruck, overwhelmed, and amused by her reaction to being in Switzer's presence; she introduces herself to the running legend and manages to squeak out a few words of admiration. I love that Menzies-Pike admits to acting the same way I imagine I would in similar circumstances.

Marathon Woman by Kathrine Switzer (Da Capo Press, 2017)

Switzer was the first woman to run the Boston Marathon as a registered runner. Using her initials on the registration form served to disguise the fact she is a woman; race director Jock Semple famously attempted to physically remove her from the race when he discovered her presence. Over the next few decades, while continuing to compete, Switzer worked tirelessly to develop opportunities for women in running and other sports. Her career as an athlete coincided with the women's rights movement of the 1970s; she played a pivotal role in laying the foundation for the road racing community that power walkers and runners benefit from today. The book culminates with Switzer serving as a member of the television broadcast team when women at long last won their hard-fought battle to compete in the marathon distance at the 1984 Los Angeles Olympic Games.

The book does not indulge in extensive personal reflection, but Switzer details enough of her inner world that the reader can understand how she made the transition from stage to stage in her athletic and personal life. I have a great appreciation for the history lesson that Switzer provides, reminding me yet again that without the generation of women before me fighting their battles I would not be able to enjoy the sport that I do now. I am also thankful that she illuminated the importance of corporate sponsors to the sport of recreational running. Switzer was a pioneer in obtaining corporate sponsorship to underwrite race expenses. I've been known to groan when a medal or race shirt features a prominent corporate logo; I now try to appreciate the fact that without the money the company provided to the race organization, the race would likely not have taken place.

Personal Record: A Love Affair with Running
by Rachel Toor (Bison Books, 2010)

Toor takes a memoir-style approach to her discovery that she not only enjoys but also is quite adept at running. She covers a wide range of topics divided into two categories: her personal journey as an adult athlete and her insights into coaching, training, and equipment. It's her writing style that sets *Personal Record* apart from books that tread similar territory; revelatory yet remote, even taut, it is memoir as written by a tightly coiled snake. She shares personal physical, mental, and emotional details while maintaining a sense of distance by employing cool, concise prose.

Toor exhibits insightful self-knowledge. She's not afraid to address her shortcomings, such as hyper-competitiveness and intellectual snobbery. She almost quits running at the beginning because she's not yet fast; she admits to hating anything at which she can't excel and that she finds it intolerable to have others witness her struggle. The book's chapters alternate Toor's development into a sub-elite runner with her practical yet still personal reflections that are presented not as a guide but simply as thoughts on her preferences and experiences.

Running Like a Girl: Notes on Learning to Run
by Alexandra Heminsley (Scribner, 2014)

Alexandra Heminsley didn't think of herself as someone with even a remote interest in physical activity. Yet as a coping mechanism for dealing with anxiety, depression, and insomnia, she decided to run the London Marathon. In *Running Like a Girl*, Heminsley shares her experience in training for and running that race, then recounts the ups and downs of her involvement with running over the next several years. The story follows a familiar arc: a woman who once enjoyed running about as a child loses that sense of freedom when she becomes a teen, allowing the perceived judgment of others to curtail her activity. Upon entering adulthood, she rediscovers the joy of running. Heminsley connects with the reader like a supportive girlfriend, sharing the experience of a naïve first-timer who knows nothing about proper gear, one who obsesses over how she'll appear to others when she's running in public. She skillfully conveys her thoughts via smatterings of dry British humor and a warm sense of self-deprecation.

The second part of the book lays out tips for new female runners that also can apply to power walkers. She provides solid information about injuries and equipment; that's presented along with tips for applying makeup for races, right down to false eyelashes and suggestions of nail polish colors. I have to hand it to Heminsley; she stays true to her book's title. While this may not be the guide to suit every woman, it can perhaps inspire some women to risk their pedicures and lace up a pair of running shoes.

Running with a Police Escort: Tales from the Back of the Pack by Jill Grunenwald (Skyhorse, 2019)

It's a different view of the running experience: specifically, it's the view from the rear of the race. *Running with a Police Escort: Tales from the Back of the Pack* follows the journey of an overweight woman who becomes determined to change her sedentary lifestyle. Grunenwald begins by targeting short races in her hometown of Cleveland, eventually attempting longer distances but always remaining a slow, non-competitive runner. The beauty of Grunenwald's book is that she makes no apologies—not for her speed (or lack thereof), not for her body size, not for the personality quirks she shares in humorous detail. She's simply who she is—she seems quite content with herself, and she invites the reader to enjoy her athletic experiences along with her.

There's a lot of good advice for prospective power walkers

throughout Grunenwald's book, cleverly tucked inside race stories. She slips a reflection on her love of finisher medals into a story about competing hungover on a snowy day, dragging herself through the race solely because she wanted that particular medal so badly. Oh, yes ... the things we do for race bling! The most poignant moment comes when, in Grunenwald's third-ever 5K race, she runs a course that starts and ends on the football field of her former high school. It's a place where she felt unpopular and unhappy; she returns triumphantly to compete on parts of the path where she was forced to run a mile every year during physical education class. Now a grown woman with greater self-acceptance, she has embraced running as both a literal and figurative path forward in her life.

Tales from Another Mother Runner: Triumphs, Trials, Tips, and Tricks from the Road edited by Dimity McDowell and Sarah Bowen Shea (Andrews McMeel, 2015)

This is a compilation of essays, reflections, and entertaining musings; the editors commissioned essays from writers who run and runners who write as well as solicited feedback from their podcast listeners and website readers. These "regular runners" share their experiences with maintaining a workout schedule (or not) while raising families and encountering the myriad challenges that life throws their way. Topics include spirituality, friendship, and goal setting; thanks to the variety of voices writing on a common central theme, the book is cohesive while providing a diversity of insights on the attendant joys and challenges of fitness, motherhood, and life.

The essays are grouped into sections with such titles as "Perspective," "Joy," and "Support." The "Ownership" section is about claiming identities that people sometimes avoid embracing because they feel they haven't earned it—a version of Imposter Syndrome. The specifics vary by author, but these women often felt that they were not "real" runners, denigrating their accomplishments to themselves and/or others. One gripe: There were several references to runners who felt like failures if they incorporated walking into their fitness program when battling illness or injury. Walking may not have been what they were aiming for, but I don't feel that it should be seen as a failure. Another section, "Case Studies," offers short answers to questions posed to a runner in each decade of life. The age-inclusive interview subjects ranged from a runner in her 20s to one in her 60s. I'm fully on board with the 65-year-old's comment about avoiding "I'm so old" conversations where people focus on bemoaning their aches and pains; it's much more uplifting to focus on the positive.

The Terrible and Wonderful Reasons Why I Run Long Distances by The Oatmeal (Andrews McMeel, 2014)

The Oatmeal, aka cartoonist Matthew Inman, might be the author I can most relate to. Much as I enjoying reading about super-talented athletes and people who reach seemingly impossible goals, here's a guy who is junk-food obsessed and takes up running so he can eat at least some of what he wants. In this graphic novel/memoir/humor book, Inman hilariously takes aim at himself, gym rats, and, well ... mostly at himself, his inherent laziness and his food obsessions. It's the most realistic thing I've ever read about running or exercise in general.

Part of Inman's schtick is a character called The Blerch, a monstrous little cherub whose sole mission is to make, and keep, Inman fat and lazy on the couch. Inman created an annual run in Washington called Beat the Blerch where competitors try to outrun a costumed Blerch while being tempted by various junk food offerings and comfy couches placed all along the race route. It was my pleasure to power walk Beat the Blerch once and it was absolutely as much fun as reading Inman's book.

What I Talk About When I Talk About Running by Haruki Murakami (Knopf, 2008)

I'm surprised it took me so many years to read this book; it's probably the most-referenced book about running that I've encountered. I suppose I held back in part because I was afraid Murakami was a "bro-lit" kind of guy and his writing wouldn't click with me; the people writing rapturous reviews of his work seemed to mostly be intensely running-obsessed young dudes. It turns out that reading this book is like having a beer with a cool new acquaintance who happens to be an extraordinary novelist with a running habit.

The first thing that struck me about Murakami's musings on running was his interchangeable usage of the terms running and jogging. Many runners are adamant that the term jogging is an insult, with its implication of slowness. I appreciated Murakami's willingness to employ the "J" word because it underscored his philosophy that running isn't about winning or being the fastest person out there; it's more about self-discovery and meeting personal goals. Then he lost my goodwill when describing a marathon where leg cramps forced him to walk the final three miles. He states, "A marathon is a running event, after all, not a walking event." I beg to differ! I understand that for someone planning to run an entire race, walking would represent failure. But there are many people for whom walking the entire 26.2 miles of a marathon is a dream and not a disappointment.

I'll forgive him for that, though, because he also does a beautiful job of addressing issues such as aging and body acceptance. He's very open about what he perceives as his personal failings so I opted to overlook the parts of the book that didn't click with me and enjoy the simple yet lyrical way he expresses his love for running.

Resources

Running/Power Walking Clubs

If you like the idea of finding friends to share your power walking journey, this is a sampling of what's out there waiting for you. Although many employ the term running, power walkers are welcomed with open arms. Here you can find training advice, group workouts, online and in-person support, and a community of new companions eager to share their enthusiasm and knowledge.

50 States Half Marathon Club (50stateshalfmarathonclub.com): If you're interested in beginning, or continuing, your own 50-state half marathon adventure, this is a group that can get you going. They offer race discounts, active private online groups, in-person race meet-ups, and an annual awards banquet to acknowledge runners and walkers who have achieved the 50-state goal. The club also offers other goals to work toward such as the 50 States Endurance Challenge, the 100 Half Marathons Challenge, and the Canadian Provinces Half Marathon Challenge.

261 Fearless (261fearless.org): Founded by Boston Marathon legend Kathrine Switzer, this global organization strives to use running and power walking as a tool to unite women of all backgrounds and abilities in living positive, healthy, fearless lives.

Another Mother Runner (anothermotherrunner.com): Here you can find training programs, a podcast, a blog, books, and a very lively social network that supports moms who run and power walk.

Black Girls Run! (blackgirlsrun.com): With a goal of encouraging Black women to develop healthy lifestyles, Black Girls Run! is a valuable resource for training programs, support, and race meet-ups nationwide.

Black Men Run (blkmenrun.com): From first time walkers to experienced runners, all men are invited to connect with Black Men Run in their mission to create a healthy brotherhood that encourages health and wellness among African American men.

Half Fanatics (halffanatics.com) and **Marathon Maniacs** (marathonmaniacs.com): Online groups dedicated to races—and lots of 'em. For power walkers intrigued by the idea of scaling ever-increasing achievement levels, these related organizations offer race discounts, signature race events (featuring optional in-person meet-ups plus special race-specific club swag), and on-course camaraderie. The websites list the criteria (number of races completed within a certain time frame) that must be met to qualify for membership.

Latinos Run (latinosrun.com): With a global audience of walkers and runners, Latinos Run provides encouragement to athletes from beginner to elite, reaching out to a community that has felt largely overlooked by the health and fitness industry.

Local running/walking stores: Many stores, such as the Fleet Feet chain, offer in-person training and get-togethers that are a great resource for those seeking fellowship and expert advice. Give your local store a call to find out where and when they meet and any requirements for participation.

Team RWB (teamrwb.org): Dedicated to bettering the lives of veterans, Team Red, White, and Blue provides opportunities for veterans to connect with their communities. Their mission is to offer vets an avenue to improve their physical health while avoiding isolation and depression, a goal achieved through fitness events, community service, and social gatherings.

Race Planning/Tracking/Other Resources

Athlinks (athlinks.com): Create a free athlete profile and you'll be able to track all of your official race results, compiling them in one handy place.

Eat Love Triathlon (eatlovetriathlon.com): A resource for fitness fans of all types (not limited to triathletes), featuring sports-based nutrition information from registered dietitian nutritionist Kathleen Oswalt.

HalfMarathons.net (halfmarathons.net): This website gives details about specific races, lists of don't miss events, and training plans along with a comprehensive race calendar.

Mainly Marathons (mainlymarathons.com): This race series runs in all 50 states, offering distances from 5K through ultramarathon. Mainly events are a wonderful way to complete several states within a short time period—meeting people, having fun, and eating great food along the way.

Medals4Mettle (medals4mettle.org): Not everyone is motivated to participate in races for the bling they bestow (I know, right?). Some people have been in so many competitions that they've run out of room to display or store their medals. Medals4Mettle is an organization that takes these unwanted awards and repurposes them as medals given to children and adults battling cancer and other life challenges.

Running in the USA (runningintheusa.com): A website that offers much more than a mere race calendar. In addition to a user-friendly general search function, check out the "Double Stater" search to come up with combinations of states within a specified number of miles and days. It makes planning multiple race weekends so much easier than performing a laborious manual search.

We Finish Together (wefinishtogether.org): Similar to Medals4Mettle, these folks will take your finisher medal, add a personal message of hope and support, and present the medal to an individual facing a daunting personal challenge.

Index

Numbers in *bold italics* indicate pages with illustrations

Index

210

Index

Index